BURDENS ON MY
JOURNEY

BURDENS ON MY
JOURNEY

An Intriguing Memoir

AUBREY C. H. BROWN JR., D. TH.

To order additional copies of this book, contact:
Xlibris Corporation
1-888-795-4274
www.Xlibris.com
Orders@Xlibris.com
67623

CONTENTS

DEDICATION

This book is dedicated to my beloved late father, Aubrey Brown Sr., the master of fatherhood, who has left an indelible impact on my life before leaving earth for glory on December 5, 2007. Especially to my faithful, loving, and caring mother, Eulalee Brown, whose love and care sustained me from the day of my birth until now, whose outstanding and dedicated Christian life led me to the Lord Jesus Christ, and from whom I believe I inherited the gift to write.

I specially want to dedicate this book to my thirteen siblings: Meritta, Avis, Elred, Lorna, Grace, Kenny, Errol, Jess, Webster, David, Wayne, Rohan, and Bevene—who have been my fortress in times of trouble, my teachers when I needed to learn, my mentors to follow, my defense when attacked by the big boys in school, and sometimes thorns in my flesh.

This book is dedicated to all born-again Christians on the pilgrim's journey everywhere.

PREFACE

I thank God the Father and our Lord and Savior Jesus Christ for giving me the courage and insight to write this book. There were days when I felt discouraged and thought about aborting the idea of writing this book. There were times when I would have thrown away my pen and paper, saying it was over, that I was through with writing. But some days were filled with great hope and cheer that one day my dream will come true. This book is my effort to share with you my life story, depicted as a man taking life's journey under heavy burdens that seemed unbearable. I accepted Jesus Christ as my personal savior as a teenager and was immediately brought to the front of the firing line of Christendom for the testing of my faith.

Recalling the day I started writing this book helps me understand the value of time and the dedication and discipline writing entails. The task was enormous, but I decided to burn the midnight oil in order to achieve my goal. I knew I had the mind and ability to write, but I needed some help, which could only come from the god of my salvation. So I decided to seek Him with all my heart and make my request known to Him. I somehow inherited this idea of writing from my mom, who is a former schoolteacher; she has always been writing essays and songs and working on some new mathematics. I often begged her to retire from that occupation, but she was determined to keep her brain engaged in the educational process.

It is my hope that this book will serve as an introduction to a deeper Christian experience to those who are in Christ Jesus. This book was written with you in mind, with an effort to share the story that shaped my life for good. I was brought up in the countryside in a very strict Christian home and spent my boyhood days on the farm, and on Sundays, it was compulsory to attend church. It is with deep heartfelt concerns for young people that this book is written. Therefore, I charge my fellow believers in Christ to continue in the warfare, despite of the burdens you bear on the journey to the heavenly city, for it won't be long when God shall come to your rescue and roll your burdens away.

My early days of Christian experiences were the determining factors of my present success in the ecclesiastical community. I was located at a very serious spiritual avenue that was often characterized as an example of the life of the Son of the Prophets and was subsequently nicknamed the Prophet. This title has become the trademark by which many of my peers identify me, even until this day. Those days of untold trials and persecution held me under severe stress and surmounting oppositions from all walks of life; but I kept my head up high, my feet firm on the ground, and my eyes on the prize before me because I knew that the god of heaven had His hands upon me and would not let me go for nothing.

Therefore, it is my hope that this book will be of help to anyone who reads it. May the story create an impact on all who have not yet known the Lord Jesus Christ as their personal savior. *Burdens on My Journey* is my way of expressing the imminent struggles that brought me to this juncture of my life and the amazing grace of God that took me all the way from despair to hope, from the valley of destruction to the mountaintop of salvation. In my young days, I have seen the hands of the Lord upon my life with strong leading and providential directions. Therefore, I have no other alternative but to follow in His footsteps for the rest of my earthly life, knowing that if He leads, I will find my way home.

It has been my esteemed joy and profound happiness to bring this book to the readers on the cutting edge of the twenty-first century. I am deeply indebted to the god of the universe for lavishing me with His eternal love and goodness and having put me into the ministry to perform the duties that are conducive to the growth and development of His church. As I recalled the day I started writing this book, I sought the Almighty God for guidance and direction for my life; and with the never-fading help, powerful teachings, and firm ethical and practical discipline of my pastor and spiritual father, the Reverend Dr. Fedlyn F. A. Beacon, I managed to overcome the onslaughts of the enemies of my soul.

To all the young Christian brothers and sisters, especially those that are single, I trust that this book will be of some help to you as you journey to the wider side of life. May you find enough insights to continue onward with Christ in the quest to fulfill your dreams and aspirations. May the Holy Spirit give you clear understanding, practical and spiritual application to your life while you diligently uncover this memoir of one man's struggle in life's intriguing journey of the Christian faith. As you read on, bear in mind that this is not a fiction, but a true story that has shaped my life into an eternal contract with the sovereign monarch of the universe.

Now I invite the readers to join me on this journey because my mind is made up, and my soul is steadfast. I am spiritually determined, intellectually inclined, and heavenly ambitious. Therefore, I will not stop at any station, ponder on earthly comfort, nor linger in the shadow of the onlookers. The race that I am engaged in is a spiritual one that leads to a victorious completion at the portals of glory; therefore, I will not back down from my holy calling, relinquish my esteem vocation, nor falter from the path of my noble predecessors because it would be unwise to exchange the office of my high calling for the field of others. For to accept the position of the president of this great country of ours or to attend to the coveted office of my native prime minister would certainly go down in history as a blatant demotion from the rank of nobility.

So let me go on preaching on this side of heaven, soliciting the Master to forgive my shortcomings, my folly, and my frailty and that when my days are ended, heaven will be recommended. For all my years of struggles will cease to be no more when upon the bank I stand and see the golden morn approaching. I fear not what men may say and do. I must hurry on and do the Master's will because I have seen a glimpse of the celestial city, and the Master beckons me to come to my home.

Aubrey C. H. Brown Jr.
January 17, 2008

ACKNOWLEDGMENTS

It is with great pleasure that I pause to express my utmost appreciation to *the girl of my dreams*, Elecia Patterson Brown—my wife, best friend, and partner for twenty-eight years, seven months, and four days—for her tremendous contribution to me during the time I was writing this book. Her never-fading effort and encouragement has helped me immensely in my quest to succeed in this project, typing the first chapter of the manuscript in its infancy stage and not forgetting those lovely cups of tea, served with love, which kept me awake during the course of the night

Special thanks to Dawnette Artwell-Morgan, who spent sleepless nights and tiresome days on the computer typing the manuscript. Thanks to Sandy Silvera, who assisted me in every aspect of the way in typing and proofreading this work.

Especially to my daughters Nadine and Charmaine, who gave me insights, corrections, constructive criticism, and courage from the time I started writing this book. And to my daughter-in-law, Raishia, who helped with the proofreading. I owe a tremendous amount of gratitude to my son, Khavil, who has been my typing tutor and technical advisor during every step of my journey and is responsible for me becoming my own typist.

To my beloved parents, Aubrey and Eulalee, for having brought me into the world and raising me with such discipline, dignity, and in the fear of God. Above all, I am indebted to the Almighty God, who has lavished me with His blessings and the privilege and ability to write this book.

INTRODUCTION

This book is not based on fiction, but is a true story of a young Christian boy who grew up on his father's plantation in the countryside of Spring Bank on the back side of the mountains of Jamaica, West Indies. Aubrey was brought up under the strictest parental guidance. He regarded is beloved late father as the master of fatherhood. The readers will soon understand that this book is more than a collection of historical events; the contents are unique, touching, and indisputable. The author wrote the story from the genuine premise of his personal experiences, with a view to assist his fellow men from all walks of life. In this book, the author's struggles in life's journey are presented as they emerged in various stages of his life. His story is interesting, touching, and provocative; it contains information that may well be helpful to the readers and could serve as a source of encouragement, which are too often absent from the most professional instructions.

In this book, one will find an example of courage, faith, and hope in some of the most difficult times of man's existence. This is the story of one man who in spite of the odds had no desire to denounce the things that almost destroyed him but found strength to withstand the test of time and overcame by the blood of the lamb and his faith in God. He is a man with a tremendous passion for the lost souls of men and the welfare of his fellow men. He is a brilliant thinker who engages himself in writing various books, poetry, stories, and songs and is a great fan of country music. Dr. Brown is a theologian in his own right, one who possesses an inquisitive mind toward the science of God. He has been an outstanding leader in the field of religion and community over the years and has walked with kings but kept his common touch.

May this book be a blessing to you as you sojourn this striking, provocative, and intriguing memoir that will captivate your entire life and change you for time and eternity. Dr. Aubrey Brown Jr. has been through the jungle of survival, climbed the mountains of distress, and crossed the stormy Jordan of life's restless sea; but in all his struggles, he kept his eyes on the cross, his mind on the Word of God, and his face set like flint toward the heavenly city, the new Jerusalem that John saw coming down from God. He kept his head above the waters of life and rode out the storms that traveled down his lonely road. His book *Burdens on My Journey* is a masterpiece of production that will serve as a road map to those who must trod the path that he has traversed during the great conflicts of his early sojourn in Christendom.

The author challenges his readers to rely on the Lord in the most difficult times of life's struggles with the knowledge that the same god who delivered him will be able to deliver others. His keen sense of understanding and wisdom gave him a clear view of man's unquenched quest for success and zeal to find happiness in a changing world. To this end, he coined this book for the purpose of encouraging his fellow men on their heavenly journey. Indeed, this true and intriguing story will serve as an archive of spiritual guidance to Christians everywhere.

It is my distinct pleasure and privilege to be acquainted with the author and to share in the ministry of Christ alongside such a gifted, esteemed servant of God, who defies the order of modern popularity in order to remain true to the calling of God upon his life. He is conscious of his divine calling and always seeks to safeguard the dignity of this sacred trust that is vested in him. He believes his gift to write comes from God, which he says he inherited from his mother Eulalee who is still writing at age eighty-Five.

The book epitomizes a journey of courage, strength, and perseverance in an era of extreme persecution, trials, and troubles, which marked out the tracks of his early Christian spiritual mountain climbing. Thus, the contemporary of his days can attest to the fact that it was the Lord who has led this writer through his unquenched, immense days of burdens that was often mingled with sorrow and tears.

Certainly, it was from these premises that Dr. Brown penned these fascinating episodes of his life with a view to give insight and hope to those who struggle with the various situational ethics of the Christian life. In this book, he uncovers his early upbringing, facing the challenge of dealing with a very stern and strict father, who oftentimes unleashed the long arm of his self-imposed political, judicial, and religious laws.

The heartbreaking departure from his native hometown to his father's birthplace taught him the values of family and relationship and the adjustment one has to make on various levels of life can either make or break an individual. Subsequently, this move turned out to be a step in the right direction because it was then that his life was transformed from an angry and boisterous lad bound for hell to a converted teenager destined for heaven.

Dr. Brown often refers to Aboukir, that place that he first despised even though he had never gone there prior to his parents' decision to send him there to school. Now it has become his Bethel, the place where he truly found God and wrestled with Him like Jacob until God brought him to a place of total reconciliation to the lordship of Jesus Christ.

It was there also that he experienced the infilling of the Holy Spirit, which brought comfort to his weary soul and led him through the dark days of his early beginnings. He will forever sing the praise of the good old Aboukir, that land that to him, which once seemed far away in a distant world unknown, has become the unforgettable place of precious memories that cannot be erased from his heaven-bound mind.

It is my joy and distinct pleasure to present this book to you, and I trust that it will be of great benefit to all who read it. May you find the path that leads to success and the comforting joy as you journey to the other side of life.

Maxine J. Welsh
Kingston, Jamaica, West Indies

Chapter One

MANY YEARS OF CHILDHOOD

I was born in the countryside in the friendly district of Spring Bank, about three miles from the capital city, Port Antonio. This was in the autumn of 1957. The ground was covered with autumn leaves; the news went out in the community that another boy baby was born to Aubrey and Eulalee Brown. This, no doubt, brought joy to the humble family; and my parents decided to name me Aubrey after my father because they thought I looked so much like him and was presumed to be the last child, which no doubt has proved otherwise as the years went by.

My parents were very young then, but strong, loving, caring, determined, yet humble. My mom was a dressmaker, and later, she qualified herself and soon become a schoolteacher. On the other hand, my father was in the construction business and, of course, was a dedicated farmer. He believed in hard work, which for him was the key to survival, and as a result of that, probably filling himself over full with hard work in order to sustain his cherished family.

Together we lived happily, my parents, five sisters, two brothers, and I, in our beautiful home near the skirt of the Blue Mountain. We experienced the cool, fresh breeze coming from the Caribbean Sea as our home was a few hundred feet above sea level, overlooking the city's harbor. Oftentimes, we would sit on the veranda, watching the various ships sailing toward the Port Antonio harbor from all over the world. These precious memories continue to live within me until this day, refreshing my thoughts as I traverse the known world, reflecting on those wonderful days of my childhood.

My dad was a very stern man; he didn't put up with nonsense. Whatever he said, he meant it. Sometimes he scared me so much; I didn't know when to talk or when to keep my mouth shut. As a child, fear gripped my heart many times when my dad came home from work in the twilight hours. It felt then like Judgment Day was near, especially if I had done something wrong that day. Dad's passwords were "Don't spare the rod and spoil the child." On the other hand, my mom was very quiet, tenderhearted, and prayerful as she was a dedicated Christian woman. Of all the things she feared most was Jehovah, whom she never ceased to teach her children about. Her watchword was "prayer"; she would always cry when she prayed for me. This brought much fear upon me many times, especially when I provoked her. She would always call my name to God in her prayer; this was very scary for me as I thought that God was going to get me then.

I was told that at four months old, my parents brought me to the house of the Lord for dedication as this was an important family tradition. It was a joy to my mom to give back little Aubrey Jr. to the Lord who gave him. In those days, this was a special occasion for the family, so everyone went to church that Sunday to witness the occasion. Rev. Wilson, the then pastor of the Love Lane Church of God, presented me to the Lord in dedication. He thought I was the chosen vessel of God as he related this prediction to my parents after praying for me.

My parents stated that I grew rapidly and with much anxiety, wanting to walk even before I could creep; and because of this, I suffered many injuries as a child. As a result of my ego to do something I saw my brothers and sisters doing, I frequently got into serious trouble, which was at most times life-threatening accidents, unknowingly to me. I never knew what was a danger to me; in fact, I always tried to experiment on the things that was more detrimental to my life—for example, trying to put my hands in a flame of fire or in a pot of boiling water, putting my toes in the dog's mouth, and even eating ripe hot peppers.

My parents thought I was maturing too fast for my age, and by the time I was ten months old, I started walking. Growing up with five sisters who did everything the boys did and two energetic brothers gave me the impetus to join the older bunch, so I matured unusually fast and was soon called the Champion. This was much to the displeasure of the older ones because by now, I was becoming the center of attraction at home, which was not necessarily for the good reasons.

By the time I was four years old, my parents had made up their minds that it was time to send me to public school; this, of course, was a great relief for them because I had become a tyrant in the family. I wanted to take on the whole world it seems, challenging my older brothers in fights. It was obvious that I was "getting out of hand," and my mom knew that trouble was near, so she started praying for me. My father had a tough time keeping his crops above the surface of the ground. My feet spelled trouble to the farm as I contemplated my first day at school in the next few weeks ahead.

Then came the morning of September; my dad breathed a long sigh of relief. Now his farm would be able to prosper once more. Off to the Bound Brook Infant School I went, accompanied by my two elder sisters; my mom shouted, "Thank God! Little Aubrey is going to school." After traveling the long and rocky road from the hills of Spring Bank to the plains of Bound Brook, my feet finally touched down on the lone corridor of my first school day. Sorrow and joy were my closest companions. Sorrow because I missed home, and joy because it was a new day of experience for me; it was the beginning of my formal education.

It took me a few weeks to settle in my new environment and to get acquainted with the children in my class. After two months in school, my presence spelled trouble for both teachers and students. I became a threat to the other children; at my age, I was said to be of an unusual character because I did things that were considered above my age-group. I was hot-tempered, uneasy, restless, and inquisitive; wanting to cross the unauthorized boundaries of the school to see what was going on behind every scene. It was during this period in my early childhood that caused some amount of concern for my parents and teachers. Daily complaints flooded my home from teachers, students, and relatives who were concerned about my behavior.

As I grew, my actions became more pronounced; my teachers were frustrated many times because of the trouble I gave them. One day, while I was at school, my principal, Mrs. Sam, out of frustration, locked me into the storeroom shortly after I had a fight with another boy. It was very dark in the storeroom. I felt like I was in hell. So to get some attention, I began to bang on the door, but to no avail; no one came to my rescue, so I decided to take the storeroom apart, opening all the bottles and pouring out the contents on the floor. The chemicals in the bottles contained deadly poisons. Pretty soon, the liquid started spreading all over the corridor, and the smell became unbearable to the nostrils of the school community, so they came to inquire from the principal what smelled so bad. By this time,

I was in bad shape, almost suffocating in the storeroom. God was on my side; when the principal came to open the storeroom's door, I was already passed out on the floor. They quickly rendered first aid, and I was revived in about twenty minutes.

I had not taken the incident seriously because I was on the go a short while after doing more forbidden things I shouldn't do. I was so rough at such a tender age that I was nicknamed Bibbipp Boy by Mr. Brandford Nelson, one of my mother's cousins who came from Norwich, a small district out of town. This name stuck with me so fast; and very soon, my brothers and sisters started to taunt me with the nickname, which brought much fatigue to my early school days.

Three years later, I was transferred to the Evelyn Parks Primary School, about four miles from home; again, it was mixed feelings for me. I was missing my old friends at the previous school I attended, and on the other hand, I was longing to go to my new school where the bigger boys were. It was a grand time for me. I enjoyed the long walk home from school each day, especially when it rained. I would end up being soaked from head to foot from walking in the rain with the other boys. Although I was a freshman in that school, I learned the ropes fast and soon joined the senior boys to form a team of gangsters to beat up smaller boys after school was dismissed each day.

There were days that I brought deep distress to my parents by not coming home from school at a reasonable time. Those were the days I spent at the nearby seaside close to my school, taking off my school clothes and oftentimes left them on the seashore for good. My parents thought my infant school days were full of troubles, but by the time I reached the Evelyn Park Primary School, I was creating havoc both at school and at home. Normally, school dismissed at three o'clock in the afternoon; but most times, I would get home at nights. My parents tried hard, and even though my dad was a rough man, that didn't stop me from breaking the rules. Many times, my parents went searching for me when I didn't come home from school on time.

By the time I reached grade two, my daily activities increased rapidly; more trouble was written in my book than one ever stops to think about. To keep me quiet, at times, my brothers would call out my nickname Bibbipp Boy aloud; then I would cry until I fall asleep. For me, education was a mere formality. I never took school seriously, but was just doing the daily routine even though my parents put out a lot to make my school days pleasant. During class time, I found time to shoot my classmates with rubber band slingshots in the back of their heads and to place pins on their chairs when they stood up for devotion, and when they would sit, they would get stuck in their buttocks. In addition to these, I hid the teachers' chalks daily and fought in class at least two times per week. My teachers then were very strict, but I found ways to get around them. I sometimes got caught doing wrong things in the classroom and received some serious punishment for my sins, but I never ceased from doing wrong as if I was destined to do so.

One bright Sunday afternoon, I watched the sun shining across my father's plantation; it was during the summer holidays, and it was customary for the children to play Dolly Pot, so I went and joined the others to have fun behind my father's house on the beautiful lawn. All my brothers and sisters were present; we decided to have church, or "play church," as we called it. My parents were religious people, so we were accustomed to religious activities. It was coincidental that I had always been asked by my elder sisters to be the preacher on these occasions, but somehow, I could not refuse the job to preach.

My seventh birthday had already passed, and I was now looking toward my eighth. I learned the full rights and rituals of church worship by then since I had to go to church every Sunday, rain or sunshine. In those days, we imitated everything we saw or heard in church to the letter. We didn't have a microphone, however; we made belief that we had one by using an empty can with a piece of card attached to it, from which we would speak from in conducting the service. When I was introduced to preach, I took the can; they cheered me along as I took my stand. As I started preaching, I shouted, "I want to be a preacher when I grow up!"

"Good, good," my mom said as she watched the proceedings. When "the church" ended half an hour later, we all went our separate ways. It was mango season, and some of the kids went under the mango trees, but I decided to lie on the green grass behind the house and had a little chat with myself lying quietly there in the meadow close by the house.

While I was lying on the grass, something strange happened to me, which I could not comprehend at all. Suddenly, I saw a man dressed in white robe descending from the sky to the place where I was lying. This man beckoned to me to come, to him. I was frightened, speechless, for a while. As far as I was concerned, I had seen a ghost, and then fear took hold of me and caused my heart to tremble like a frenzied man in war. I was very scared, afraid to move or to stay still, not knowing what was going to befall me; but I later learned through the word of prophecy from a preacher that the man I saw was the Lord, calling me to the work of the ministry. This was a strange and awful experience for me that evening. I then ran as fast as I could and hid myself under my mother's bed, trembling with fear. This was an unusual experience for me, which left me terrified, sweating with great fear until I eventually fell asleep.

It was not long afterward that my sisters found out that I was missing and decided to search for me. They searched all over the plantation, in every bedroom of the house, the kitchen, and the bathroom, but still did not find me. My parents got worried, and my brothers and sisters too. There were elements of frustrations in my family, coupled with fear for my life. They thought of filing a report to the police on the matter, but there were mixed feelings about this, and the idea was aborted immediately. My mom was a determined person, so another search was launched to find me before night fell. After hours of meticulous searching, my mom found me under her bed, fast asleep, snoring away in dreamland as the previous visitation of the spirit-being preoccupied my subconscious. There was rejoicing that evening in the family because their son and brother were found. I never uttered a word about my experience until after many years when I was converted to Christianity.

The remaining days of my primary school life had the teachers on their toes, looking out for trouble from me daily. I knew my days at the Evelyn Parks School were numbered. A gloom of unpleasantness began to haunt me as I thought of that moment to come, when I shall bid farewell to my teachers and schoolmates. It seemed felt like lumps of heaviness were in my heart as I reflected on the past few years of primary school life. The tears came rolling down as I walked slowly into the nearby park, meditating on the future of my life and the memories of the past.

The long and hot summer holiday came, and I felt a sense of freedom from the classroom's activities. But on the other hand, I could not escape the day-to-day labor of my father's plantation. It was like punishment for not being in school. By this time, I had just turned twelve and was looking forward to "big school" in September, where I would rub shoulders with the older boys even though I was very small in stature.

For me, it was the hardest summer, filled with sweat and tears; my father intensified our daily duties and told me he was preparing me "to wear long pants," meaning "making me into a man." I thought becoming a man was too hard a job, yet the idea of becoming a man had always been my joyful expectation. By so doing, I would escape the terror of my father's whip, but time has proven that there was no easy street out of my father's kingdom of self-proclaimed parental laws. That summer had left both pleasant and unpleasant memories in my mind, from the freedom from schoolbooks and classroom experience to the harsh lashes of my father's whip to the unending labor in the plantation.

One wondered if that summer would ever come to an end. The boys and girls alike toiled in the heat to prepare coconut and bananas for export. There was no easing up. Dad was of course the boss who gave the orders, and we were to be careful that none were broken. Mom was easygoing as usual, taking care of the household activities on a daily basis, but Dad ruled with an iron fist the terrains of the home and property. When he spoke, I sometimes trembled like a man with the fear of death; his voice rose like that of Goliath, the giant, and brought much fear upon me for the greater part of my childhood days.

Thank God, summer ended; my elder sister Jean took me to the senior school and had me enrolled. I had just gone to the untrained, under the tree Barber, in the person of my father, prior to going to big school. I had to keep it quiet, not allowing anyone to know that my dad was the barber, or else you would hear the end of that story sooner or later. One could tell it was a novice that had practiced the trade of barbering on my head as a result of the unprofessional look on the head of a September's morning schoolboy. I had to wear a cap for many days in order to keep the big boys from playing drums on my head; but you could not tell my father that he was a contractor and a farmer, but not a barber, or else he would serve notice on you to attend to his self-made whip of prolonged lashes across my weary back.

The new haircut brought tears to my eyes not only because it was not professionally done; but the big boys took control of my shiny head and used it as a target practice for their cracker balls, slingshots, and musical drum set. Not to mention my khaki suit, well starched by my mom for days and pressed with razor-sharp seams, which appeared like I was in straightjacket. The shoe I wore to school was the most modern of the time—the Tarzan, a shoe made solely from rubber. I had to wear it to school at summertime in a ninety-degree Caribbean temperature. It was very difficult for me at first because I was just getting used to wearing shoes because in the earlier years of my childhood, my parents could not afford to buy me a pair; in fact, shoes were seen as luxury in those days and were only worn when going to church or on very special occasions. So I needed a little time and practice in my first Tarzan shoes in order to make the necessary adjustment from bare footedness to shoe wearing.

Although very small in stature, my heart was big; I wanted to resist the big boys who were taunting me day after day. Vengeance was in my heart, so I stayed up late at nights, planning ways of getting even with the boys at senior school. Three weeks passed since I started big school, and it was then that I began a career of vengeance. I was fighting without fear at least once per day. I decided to make myself known to the teachers and students that I was a boy of destructive temperament. The headmaster (principal) broke many canes on my back; and when I escaped his lashing, he would send the big boys to pursue me, but most times to no avail because I outran them all. I was smaller than most boys in my age-group but was not afraid to defend myself when it came to the test.

I was a keen sportsman, very much a part of every game that was played at senior school: cricket, football, tennis, just to name a few. I was so much into sports to the extent that I would forsake classes in order to play a game of cricket or football. As an ardent sportsman, I managed to gain a place in my house team and ultimately in the school cricket team as a fast bowler and batsman, and I even captained my class team at times. Cricket was like music in my bones; and I made it my first occupation, above all others, including my secondary education, which no doubt brought some amount of fatigue to my beloved mother. At the same time, it boiled the anger of my father to its greatest intensity, which led him to the new self-invented form of higher education called Licks in Time and Licks In Case, which simply meant that if I was neglecting my education, he would beat it into me with the cracking of his whip until I have learned all that there was in at every subject in senior school. This marked the beginning of my new nightmare, "the encounter of my father's method of education"; he then revised his vengeance of fatherhood with a view to correct my false notion of education in his school of parental fury.

Notwithstanding the great love I had for the sports of the day, I always kept in focus the impending wrath of my dad but still found time to breathe out threats of anger and injuries to my fellow schoolmates to the point where I almost damaged the future of my senior school education. Nothing seemed to detour me from the paths of mischief; it seemed I was possessed with a spirit of destruction with an intention to put out the lives of others. Unusually, school would dismissed at three thirty in the afternoon; but for me, the night would have to fall before I leave the sports ground at Halifax Pavilion. Every so often, spectators from all strata of society would stop at the pavilion on their way home from their jobs to watch a game of cricket. This, for me, was the greatest time of my day. I yearned for the opportunity to display my ability to play the game of cricket. The people cheered when I hit a ball from the electrifying fast bowler Horace Davis to the extra cover boundary for four runs, or when I hooked top bowler Maurice Campbell over midwicket for a six. My mind was fastened to the game of cricket like Crazy Glue, not allowing anything to distract me by any means, and so I lavished myself in the game to the thrill of the spectators when I uprooted the stumps of the classical batsman Edger Watson with one of my fast-moving deliveries from the northern end of the pavilion.

It was the bloom of my school days; my love for cricket had become somewhat religious because I would give up everything for it, including school. The quest for excellence in cricket was on the forefront of my mind; school had now taken the second place in my life. I was located on a very acute angle of popular misleading, hoping to represent my country in this beloved game of glorious uncertainties, but my parents had other things in mind for me; and my dad, in particular, was concentrating on increasing his search in Cooper's Hill for more supply of Swibble jack whip for the purpose of straightening out of my crooked wrongdoings with merciless lashes across my back. It was regular practice for me to get home late and even sometimes at nights from school because of my love for cricket. My mom started to get curious and was very concerned about my actions and activities, so she asked my dad to check up on my activities at school. The following day, a cricket match was scheduled to be played at the Halifax Pavilion, between my school and the Titchfield High School. As a member of my school team, I deemed it my pride and privilege to represent my school, and my love for cricket could not allow me to miss this historic match. The match began shortly after school dismissed at 3:30 p.m.; hundreds of spectators gathered to see this event. While the match was in progress, my father was coming from work on his bicycle; when approaching the pavilion, he heard the crowd shouting and cheering. So he stopped for a while to see what was happening. To his surprise, it was his son, yours truly, at the batting crease, hitting the bowlers all over the pavilion, to the spectators' delight. He stood in a moment of shock and wonder as he quietly watched me delighting the crowd with an array of brilliant strokes "Fine boy! Fine cricketer" shouted Mr. Dennis Atkinson of the Halifax Sports Club, who was standing next to my father. My dad nodded his head and smiled with humble pride to hear such nice words about his son, then quickly mounted his bicycle and sped away home.

The match ended with my team being victorious over the Titchfield school team. I was undefeated on forty-three runs, including three sixes and five fours in what my captain called "a splendid knock of victory." The excitement was now over, the glorious cricket match had ended, and the twilight was fast approaching. The jubilant team was celebrating when a sudden gloom of sadness came over me; the thought of facing my parents' anger was now haunting me like demons sent to kill. I carefully planned a lie and practiced it on my way home, "that my teacher gave us extra lesson for that evening because exams were coming up soon." This I thought would be the most appropriate lie to tell my parents since it was the time of final exams at school, so I felt secured and had great hope that I was going to escape the long arm of my father's law.

Upon reaching home, I greeted my parents with the usual greeting: "Good evening, Mom. Good evening, Dad."

"Good *night* you mean, master," my father replied angrily.

I suspected trouble immediately; somehow, my father had a way of knowing when I'm lying, but this time, he had a firsthand knowledge of where I went after class was dismissed. I had not the slightest idea that my father was in the crowd at the pavilion watching me that evening. In addition to this, he went to my school that day to investigate my activities; unfortunately, I had no knowledge about this then. So I insisted on my story, trying to convince him, not knowing I was adding fire to his fury. He commanded me to go change my clothes and prepare to cook dinner. By this time, I thought dinner was ready because I was hungry too, but this was not to be. While I was changing my clothes, my father pounced upon me with a piece of Swibble jack whip he prepared for me a few hours before over the fire, which was his way of preserving the whip. The first lash across my back left me scampering for cover; then more and more it came like floods of rain upon dry, thirsty land. He hit me everywhere. I could feel it with massive strokes from the whip, and he let me know each time the reason for his lashing. My back was on fire as the lashes increased. I found an open door and escaped with a "running lash"; this was the last lash, but hotter than the previous ones, which left my back feeling like it was on fire.

Next day was the earliest I've ever come home from school; my back was still in pain from yesterday's horror of vengeance, but I pretended I had changed for the better. Instead, I grew worse, and flogging became my daily routine. I started a new campaign of terror—throwing stones on the people's housetops in my community and shattering their glass windows too, shooting dogs with "slingshots," and disturbing various church services, especially the Pentecostal churches. I would block public roads with fallen trees and debris for fun, inconveniencing motorists and pedestrians. New Year's Eve was the heyday of my disorderly conduct as I joined with my smaller brothers to overturn garbage containers in the streets, break public streetlights, puncture car tires, kill the neighbors' dogs, and set alight private and public properties on fire, especially churches.

I was at the height of a career in vandalism; one New Year's Eve night, as I continued my evil activities, a police patrol car came upon me suddenly, shortly after I blocked the Spring Bank Road. They were about to arrest me, but I told them, "I came on the scene a short while ago, found out the road was blocked, and was volunteering to clear it." Somehow, one of the cops believed my story, but another doubted; luckily for me, one of my cousins, Sergeant Stanley Brown, a member of the police party, recognized me that night. I was let off the hook only after I was ordered to clear the road. Otherwise, I would be arrested; and my tragic tale would be told to my father, who would have taken me close to the gates of hell. However, shortly after the police party departed, I blocked the road again and fled the scene.

The following day was Sunday; my sister Elred and I went to the Pentecostal church. The saints were singing, jumping, and speaking in tongues. I sat quietly at the back row of the church, watching and listening carefully, but not understanding what was happening. I thought to myself, *these folks are crazy people.* So I began mocking and jeering those who were in the Spirit. A devilish thought came to me; then I took out my elastic rubber band, made some paper shots, and began shooting those people that were said to be in the Spirit on their buttocks, then bowed my head as if I was praying. Prior to this, my sister saw me once misbehaving and reprimanded me strongly, but I continued doing bad things in church until the service ended.

On our way home that night, I remember thinking about those crazy folks in church and was laughing loudly on the street when suddenly; Mr. Charles Brown's dogs jumped over his high fence and started tearing me apart. I had just bought the new pair of pants I had on, and the dogs destroyed it utterly and bit me all over my body like angry lions devouring their prey. They rushed me to the general hospital for treatment where I received three injections and other medication. My sister told me firmly that this was a sign from God for what I had done at church, and to add to my fury, those were the same dogs I often shot with my slingshot when passing at nights. It was a sure warning to me to make an end of my dog-killing career, but instead, this incident marked the beginning of sorrow for all the dogs in the community as I hunted them down with merciless vengeance and with the intention to kill them all.

Soon, I was well again and back on the street with a new fixed intention to kill any dog that came my way; and not many days after, the same dogs that bit me met their untimely death at my expense. I waited patiently for revenge and murdered them all. It was then that my hatred for dogs began to intensify; my father's own dog broke the law and ate my neighbor's chicken. I ran him down, held him, pronounced Flip guilty, passed the verdict, and hanged him upon a cocoa tree behind my father's house.

My devastating era soon became the deep concern of the neighborhood as many complaints were reaching my parents daily about their son Aubrey Jr. Cursing indecent language was a norm for me; sometimes I cursed until it seemed like the atmosphere became black like midnight before my eyes. I was very hot-tempered, and oftentimes when flogged by my father,

I would retaliate by cutting down his plantation with a sharp machete. When my elder brothers and sisters spoke to me strongly or whip me for any wrongdoings, I breathed out threats to kill them all. There was a spirit of deep arrogance and intolerance in me, which was controlling my life. In those days, my mom never stopped praying for me that God would change my life at that tender age.

In the absence of my father, I seized the opportunity to reign terror at home; my mom had nervous breakdown from dealing with my behavior. I used to kick a football in the house, breaking glasses and windowpanes, which disturbed my sick mother, causing her heartache and pain. One day, my mom sent me to the shop to buy a pound of salt fish. I returned after five and a half hours with about half a pound of salt fish. She noticed that the salt fish seemed to be less than one pound, so she inquired of me what had happened to the other portion, and I told Mom a cow chased me, and I lost a portion of the fish. The truth was I ate half of the fish along the road, not thinking that anyone will find out; but unfortunately, my sins caught up with me.

My father came home and was told about the incident; he proceeded promptly to investigate the matter. He brought the fish to me and said, "How much fish is this, master?"

I replied, "I don't know, Dad. That's all Mr. Sam gave me."

"Are you sure, sir?" asked my father.

"Yes, yes, Dad," I replied.

"Okay sir," he said. "We are both going to see Mr. Sam right now," he added. "And we will bring the salt fish too," he continued. My heart began to beat faster than normal because I knew my father was a man of his word. So off we went to Mr. Sam's shop, three and a half miles away. I was walking quietly behind my father, planning how to defend myself when getting there.

Upon reaching the shop, Mr. Sam recognized me straightway; looking at my face, he knew something had gone wrong. "What can I do for you, Mr. Brown?" asked Mr. Sam.

My father answered, "How much salt fish did you sell this boy today?"

"One pound! One pound exactly," said Mr. Sam. "What's the problem?" he added.

"This is all he brought home," replied my father, throwing down the salt fish on the counter angrily.

"I'm sure I gave him one pound of salt fish, Mr. Brown, and I have a witness to prove it too," Mr. Sam replied

"OK, OK, Mr. Sam, that's all I needed to hear," said my father. "I'll see you tomorrow," he added as he walked away holding on to my shirt firmly.

I was sweating rapidly in the cool evening, not only because I was embarrassed, but also because I knew that my mom, brothers, and sisters were waiting eagerly at home for the result of this matter. Fear gripped me as I trod home under the long arm of my father's strong punishment. Upon reaching home, my father began to put on the whip to my back without reservation; by this time, the others realized that I was guilty of stealing the salt fish even though my father had not said a word to them. The cracking of the Swibble jack whip across my back must have sounded like the rifles of frenzied men at war to the nearby neighbors, who came scampering down the alley in an attempt to rescue me from the long arm of my father's punishment. My brothers and sisters watching the episode were silent, yet in much amusement as the flashing whip moved up and down from the sky to my bruising back. The lashes were too numerous to count, too powerful to escape, too direct to resist; then at the end, the whip had fallen apart, and that's when my nightmare came to an abrupt end. From that day forward, I was nicknamed Fish the Bitch.

It seemed I was on a journey destined for trouble at all costs and never seemed to be able to control my own life. Flogging had become a part of my life, and even then, I grew worse as many of my father's Swibble jack whips broke upon my stubborn back in my years of childhood and left me with haunted memories of youthful days.

My mother's sorrow increased on a daily basis because of my childhood actions, which caused her much pain within her heart. But Mom never stopped praying for me that God would save me from my sins and set me free; she was convinced that if God didn't save me, something dangerous was going to befall me soon. She was always singing, "Rock of Ages, cleft for me. Let me hide myself in Thee." Her prayers brought much fear upon me, and the wrongs I committed in the past kept haunting me in my sleep like a ghost. It was then that I knew the prayer of one person could affect the lives of others. As my mom prayed, my behavior was gradually changing, and I was becoming more and more interesting in the things that pertaineth unto God. Time had started to catch up on me, and I began to examine my own life. I was now looking down the road of time, and my thirteenth birthday was imminent; as a young lad, the fear of God took a hold on my life and would not let me go for nothing. Mom was a role model to me; she kept praying, singing, and praising God in the home as if she was leaving for heaven the next day. I was locating in an actual quiet avenue of my life—the turning point from terror to tears, from anger to peace, from hot-temperedness to a spirit of real calm. With just two more years to go at the senior school, I actually pondered in my mind whether to accept Christianity or continue in my old ways. It was a great struggle within me. I thought about my schoolmates, how they would accept me if I became a church boy; confusion was the main subject of my days that particular time in school. My mom took me to church the following Sunday; the service was rich and rewarding. Then I was becoming convinced about this "God business."

A month passed by, and my family and friend noticed that there was a gradual change in my behavior; the first evidence was a quiet calm in whatever I was doing, which was very unusual to most people who knew me. The truth is, something was beginning to happen in my life; the Lord was taking over from the devil that haunted me in the past. The Reverend Roland McNally, pastor of the Love Lane Church of God who oftentimes prayed that God would change me, discovered that indeed a serious transformation was in progress in my life and immediately became an integral part of that change. Mom's joy began to multiply as her son was inching closer to the god of her salvation.

Soon, I joined the new convert's class at the church after, responding to the preacher's invitation to discipleship. This was a positive move in the right direction, and my relatives' hearts began to rejoice with great joy. I was encouraged by the pastor on numerous occasions to serve the Lord as my personal savior. So not long afterward, I became a prime candidate for water baptism and a prospective youth leader in the church at Love Lane.

It was now the second year of my senior school days, and then something happened at school that changed my life from wrong to right. It was this incident that marked the new chapter in my decision making for Christ. One brilliant Friday afternoon, my fellow students and I were playing a friendly cricket match on the school ground when tragedy struck the school community. Unfortunately, I was the center of this unfortunate incident that changed my life for good. I was at the batting crease; the bowler was Horace Davis. My classmate produced a fast-rising delivery on my leg stump. I made one of the most extravagant hook shot off my legs in an attempt to pull the fast bowler to the backward square leg boundary.

Unfortunately, I only succeeded on landing a powerful blow in the right eye of the wicket keeper, Michael Small, who was standing up close behind the stumps. It was an almost fatal blow to his right eye, which rendered him unconscious on the ground. He was rushed to the public general hospital in a serious condition and was later transferred to the university hospital in the capital. The doctor reported later that his eye pupil could not be found, and so surgery was imminent. This was one of the worse days of my childhood. The cricket match ended prematurely on a sorrowful note; there was a gloom of sadness on my face and a lump in my throat as I left the cricket ground with my head hanging down in deep distress.

I kept the incident quiet from my parents for months; my heart was aching within me for fear that this tragic tale will be told someday, and my world will then be turned upside down when at last it reaches my father's ears. After several months of silence, I tried to forget about that sad day at school; meanwhile, Michael's parents struggled with medical bills and various trips to the specialists. It was my hope that the news of the incident would soon be forgotten, and Michael's eye will be better again. This I thought would give assurance that the news will never get to my parents, especially my dad; but soon, my wishful thinking was about to be turned into a day of unpleasant surprise that could scare the life out of me.

That day finally came at an uncertain hour when up the steep hills to our home came Michael and his parents accompanied by a lone policeman, who was tall, witty, stout looking, and had his gun within its shield. By the look of the lanky lawman, it seemed as if he came up the hill to make a kill. I was nervous as could be as they came close to the veranda. I noticed that Michael's right eye was covered with a medical bandage. My parents knew immediately something had gone sour from the sight of the lanky lawman. Mrs. Small, Michael's mother, introduced herself to my parents, and straightway, my mom recognized that Mrs. Small was her uncle's daughter. I rushed into my room and locked the door because I knew I was in trouble, and the presence of the policeman drove fear in my heart. Mrs. Small then explained everything concerning the incident to my parents, then presented the doctor's report concerning Michael's eye and the medical bills to be paid.

My father remained calm and cool after hearing everything, then called me with a strong voice, "Come out here, boy! Let me hear from you what happened." I was trembling with fear as I walked slowly to the place where they were sitting. I looked at Michael, and he looked at me, and then the tears began to fall from my eyes as I tried to explain the incident that took place at school on that sad Friday afternoon.

It was a somber and penitent afternoon for all of us, but it was that tragic incident that brought long-lost relatives together again. Michael and I hugged each other. I told him how sorry I was for what had happened, and he forgave me and said, "It was an accident, Aubrey, not your fault. Maybe I was too close behind the stumps where you were batting on that day."

It was that moment that brought our friendship closer and changed the course of my life. My parents agreed to help defray the cost of Michael's medical bills. Although Michael never regained his proper vision, he was able to move on in life and continue the friendship we had in our cherished schoolboy days. We later graduated together from the senior school with great pride and joy, endeavoring to keep the ties that bound our friendship together in all our years of childhood. Tears gushed out of my eyes as I walked through the gate of the senior school, leaving the many teachers and friends behind with precious memories in my bosom, for those were the years of my childhood days.

The Old Home Scene of my Childhood

CHAPTER TWO

DEPARTURE FROM HOMELAND

The final two years in senior school and especially that incident on the cricket field drove me closer to the Lord Jesus Christ. I placed myself in Michael's situation and saw my own eye lying flat and lifeless on the ground. This drove me nearer to God. Even though I was not yet baptized, I was becoming more and more committed to the work of the Lord at the Love Lane Church of God.

My interest was centered in the youth department, a vital ministry in the church; and soon, I became an integral part of the church activities. During that period, I got a job at the Sang Hing Supermarket as a price controller and was earning six dollars per week. The job was paying good dividend, so I felt comfortable. But my future education was uppermost in my parents' minds, so they constantly urged me to go back to school because for them education was paramount for their children, and I was cognizant of this stubborn fact. But I kept on working with a view to erase the idea of going back to school from my mind and with the hope that my parents will soon stop nagging me about such important matter.

After working for two years, my parents thought it was time for me to quit the job and get on the road for school again. On the other hand, I was holding on firmly to the job, much to the displeasure of my parents, who believed that education should come first. After several weeks of serious thinking, I finally decided to give up my job and prepare to return to school. It came as a real surprise when my parents told me that my new school was the Aboukir Educational and Industrial Institute in the Garden Parish of St. Ann. I was very disappointed to the point where I felt some amount of depression in my spirit, knowing I had to depart from my homeland to my father's birthplace to live and attend school.

The school was located approximately 121 miles from home; it seemed like a foreign land across the sea to me because I had never left home before to live anywhere and had never traveled more than twenty miles in any direction from my parents' home. This was one of the most frightening circumstances of my seemingly unending school days. I soon learned of the struggles and hardship I was to expect and not to mention the seven-mile journey to school each day from my proposed new home in Maida to the illustrious Aboukir Educational and Industrial Institute, where great men and women of previous generations had studied at the feet of noble lecturers.

I was totally devastated after listening to my brother Errol sharing his experience as a recent graduate of the same school and was now a police officer assigned to the Denham Town Police Station in the capital city. The days ahead were filled with passive aggression in regard to my departure from home; never in my life had there been such fear, anxiety, and procrastination. There were sleepless nights, nightmares, and doubts that haunted me as I waited for January's morning to arrive. There were times of discouragement, tear, and even anger as the day approached. The thought of leaving parents, brothers, sisters, friends, and church folk brought great drops of tears to my eyes as I tried to wash away the memories of leaving.

It was now noised abroad that my departure was at hand, so my friends and relatives came by to cheer me along. It seemed as if I was going to a foreign land; the journey sounded like a couple of days' travel in my mind. The tears came voluntarily as the days drew near. On January 2, my suitcase was packed; my spirit was sad. The time finally came for me to go. The reopening of school was on January 6, and my parents were praying that I had no tricks because whether I liked it or not, they meant I had to go.

The next day was my departure; it was in the early-morning hours, and the ground was covered with frost and dew from the overnight sprinkling from above. It was very cold outside as I bid farewell to my beloved family and began my journey to another side of the world, not knowing what will befall me there. But I mustered courage from above and rested in the fact that my brother-in-law Keith was with me to take me to that sacred land of my father's birth where these feeble feet had never trod before. Keith was originally from Aboukir, so I was in good hands, with confidence that we would find our way to that new land. So there my new journey began with great expectation, from the Blue Mountain's skirt to the Garden Parish on the northern coast of the island.

For me, it was the first experience traveling on a big bus; it was called the Honey bee, a fifty-one-seat public passenger bus that seemed to stop for every person that was on feet even though it had almost two times the legal seating capacity on board already. The bus was packed like sardine in a tin, but the driver continued to stop for more passengers. Passengers disembarked, and others embarked continuously along the route for the duration of the journey. Soon, fatigue crept into my already stressed mind and caused me to become restless, upset, and, even at times, bitter. I tried to catch a breath of fresh air from outside, but the packed bus of rough, sweaty passengers clustered the small space I was occupying and almost stifled the life out of me.

There were moments when I felt some amount of excitement within me as the beautiful scenery captured my attention when some of the passengers got off at different intervals. It was then that I had the opportunity to see the outside for brief moments; but soon, others came on board momentarily, and we are in for a squeeze again. The best time for me was when the bus traveled at rapid speed on a distant highway out of the residential areas. I knew then that there will be no passengers on the highway to pick up, so I would breathe a sigh of relief. The journey became tiresome at times, and I got restless and uncomfortable after traveling for so long. We passed various ancient and historical sites along the way on our marathon journey to that far land of my father's birth. Keith tried to educate me as we passed the historical sites of my ancestors, but my spirit was very low; my mind was fixed on home where the heart knows, the joy bell rings, and the roses never fade.

As we traveled, the sudden realization came upon me that I was getting farther and farther from my homeland. Suddenly, a lump of sorrow came in my heart, and tears had the better part of my journey to the place called Aboukir. The silence was broken by the teardrops from my eyes. There was much effort to restrain myself from the memories of home, but it became more and more unbearable for me to forget, so I went on weeping toward the final destination. Keith tried to cheer me up as we traveled, but nothing seemed to ease the pain I bore and heal the sorrow within my bosom. I was not at all together; my heart broke in a thousand pieces. I remembered

Mama, how she would call me to her bedside at night and pray for my soul to sleep. My dad was my hero, and my siblings were my playmates, and now I was gone so far from them; it broke my heart every mile of the way. For the most part, I felt like I had gone from my loved ones forever, sentenced to a far land with no hope of returning. But Keith lifted my spirit with words of encouragement as we journeyed to the land of my father's birth. He assured me that things were going to get better when I see that fair land and promised me that I would not regret living there. It was only then that a ray of hope came over my sad spirit.

After passing numerous winding roads and narrow bridges, Keith indicated to me that we were nearing home. A sense of joy came over me; a chance had come to experience my father's homeland for myself. Wondering what Aboukir was like, I waited with eager eyes to see the land that would become my future home. The huge bus came to a halt at the Aboukir bus stop. Keith said, "We are home free, brother."

I thought, *Maybe free, but not home.* And I pondered. To my surprise, it was the beginning of another journey; only this time, it was a shorter one, in a smaller bus, seven miles ahead over steep hills and rocky road. "Are we not in Aboukir?" I inquired of Keith.

"Yes, brother," he replied. "But there are more than one Aboukir," he added; then he smiled and said, "There is Aboukir Road, Top Aboukir, and Bottom Aboukir. We are going to Bottom Aboukir, brother." My heart sunk with grief when he spoke these words to me.

Now I was in deep regret, wondering why I had to leave my home. "I've never traveled such hills and valley before," I told Keith.

"You haven't seen anything yet. We have just begun the journey," he replied seriously. My sorrow began to multiply; my heart was aching with pains as he spoke those words. As we journeyed, I found some courage in the phrase my mother often used, "If you want good, your nose will have to run." So I proceeded with this in mind and with my mind set on school and the prayers of my mother as we traveled toward Bottom Aboukir, the place soon to be called home. There were a thousand thoughts in my mind going down the rocky road of Aboukir. I asked myself many questions of which I had no answers. I was a prisoner of my own self, a prodigal from a distant land, who, for some strange and unknown reason, was banished to another land of unchartered course for the purpose of solidifying his quest for higher education and to reveal his undiscovered intellect. But for me, this was a trip to hell with no hope of returning. Darkness was over me, and I could not see the light of day from the premise I stood, and I wondered if my God-given parents had made the right decision.

We traveled for about half an hour on the rocky stone road, and then we came to a smoother paved road toward the homestretch. I took courage even though I was tired and weary from the painstaking journey, knowing that the end was in sight and that my new home was a few miles away. Soon, we finally reached that far-fetched place where I must, in a few moments, call home and dwell until my school days be over. Then upon that glad tomorrow, I should claim success and venture upon my return to that native land of my birth. Upon entering my brother-in-law's house, we knelt down and prayed as was the usual custom, thanking God for journeying mercies and providential care. It was a refreshing evening of welcome, introduction, and greetings. I finally met Keith's parents, Mass Sill and Aunt Daughta as they were affectionately called. We then had dinner together and chatted for a while; there, I began to feel at home for the first time that evening.

The community was very quiet and lonely except for a few young men smoking ganja by the roadside. Twilight was near at hand, the breeze blew cold across the Aboukir woods, and then the rain came tumbling down as if a welcome signs to a newcomer. It was the coldest climate I ever experienced that night in my life. I was freezing under the huge blanket. It was a night of torment and nightmare for me as the thought of facing the daybreak and the journey to school the following Monday kept lingering in my mind. I tossed and turned all night, thinking of home and family. The new climate brought some amount of fear in me because my hometown had always been pretty warm, and now I was experiencing unexpected cold weather. For Keith, this was normal weather; but for me, it felt like winter in England.

The next day was Saturday. I rose up early from sleep, very anxious to view the community and to meet some new relatives. The atmosphere was very cloudy; thick fog bleared my vision of the houses around, and I could hardly see the main road, which was close to the house. Anxiety had a firm grip on me while awaiting a glimpse of the morning sun. Eventually, the sun came out at about nine o'clock, shining through the gloom and brightening my depressed spirit. That Saturday was an interesting day; I had the privilege of touring the communities of Aboukir and Maida and met many of my relatives. Then at evening, when the sun went down, it was time to prepare for church the following day and school the next day. So with much anticipation, I looked forward to the days ahead, with hope and faith in God, who has helped me thus far.

Sunday morning came; it was time for church, so everyone was up early preparing for Sunday school, which was mandatory for all church members in those days because this was an integral part of the church's education program. On reaching the church, I was placed in the young people's class by my articulate brother-in-law Keith Wray, who invited me to church that day. It was a very interesting Sunday school lesson as I recalled, and the golden text was taken from the book of Hebrews 10:22. "Let us draw near with a true heart in full assurance of faith, having our hearts sprinkled from an evil conscience, and our bodies washed with pure water." The lesson was based on the Mosaic Law, represented as a shadow of the things to come. This was my first Sunday school class in a Pentecostal church; but at the end of the class, an indelible impact was left upon my heart, which remains until this day.

After the Sunday school ended, the morning's service began at 11:00 a.m. sharp, with singing and worshipping, hand clapping and feet stamping. I felt out of place in that atmosphere, being in a Pentecostal church for the first time. The style of worship was different from that of my home church; the saints back home were more on the quiet side, but somehow, I became fascinated with this type of worship. The people seemed to enjoy what they were doing; so I started clapping my hands too, trying to catch on to the new way of worship in that old-fashioned church at Maida, which later turned my world upside down. A warm and friendly welcome was given to each visitor; then the energetic Spirit-filled moderator Sister Blossom singled me out in the large crowd as Keith's brother-in-law from the Blue Mountain parish of Portland. She informed the congregation that I came to take up residence in Aboukir and that I was a prospective student for the Aboukir Institute. You could tell from the look on Sister Blossom's face that she was a former student of that noble institution. The vast crowd turned their attention toward me while she was speaking, and an enthusiastic welcome drove a humble homeboy into an instant celebratory mode that would change his life forever.

The morning's service ended, leaving a creative psalm of peace upon my heart, and a rich rewarding potion of blessing was lavished in my fragmented life. My disturbed soul of religious complications was indicted in a good matter. There was an unusual moment of rejoicing in my heart as the Spirit-filled saints of Maida New Testament Church of God greeted, hugged, and kissed me as if I was sent from heaven. I suddenly felt a sense of belonging; the cheerful people of God treated me with much love, which drove me closer toward the god of my salvation. I walked home from church that day with springs in my steps because my burdens were gone, and a sense of joy lingered in my heart as I walked the rocky road home from the church.

Reminiscing on the service, I felt that my time was near at hand to make God the sovereign ruler of all my undertakings. I continued to focus on a bright future in the Christian faith with a view to learn as much as I can from those who were placed over me in the Lord. After dinner, I went to sleep, still tired from the long travel of the past day. When I awoke a few hours later, I was ready to go to church again; for some strange reason, I had a great urge to discover more of God and His Word, which was very unusual for one like me who, in times past, was a persecutor of the church of God. However, by seven o'clock, I was up and ready to go, perhaps driven by the compulsion of the morning's service and the warmth of the people of Maida.

The evening service was packed out, with all seats taken; this, to me, was unusual because in my hometown, the people seldom attend night services unless there was a special function held in the church. Now I had to learn a new culture from the people of the Garden parish. Notwithstanding, I was willing to divest the culture of myself in order to accommodate another. I was possessed with a spirit of enthusiasm, anxious to reach church in order to hear those refreshing songs of Zion that I had heard for the first time. The church was a few furlongs away from home, so for me, that was absolutely convenient; this no doubt gave me no excuse to be absent from church. We reached church very early that evening; the old-fashioned saints were singing some lively songs with loud music ringing out in the neighborhood. Brother Prophet was on lead guitar, and oh! What an evening it was—hand clapping, feet stamping, hallelujah shouting, and tongue talking. It was a mystery at Maida on that fair Sunday of Pentecostal demonstration, and I was the conscientious observer, sitting on the fence of modern Pentecostalism not knowing which of the Christian denomination to embrace.

Rev. James Walden was the host pastor; he was short, dark, and stocky and wore a bright, pleasant smile. After the youth choir sang, the reverend gentleman took his stand and began to speak with much conviction. The Spirit was upon him heavily as he began to preach; one could tell that the Holy Spirit was manifesting in him from the way he spoke the Word of truth. He moved from one place to the other as he delivered an expository sermon of Gospel deliberation. As he continued to demonstrate the scriptures in an articulate fashion, then came spontaneous shouts of praises to God; this sent chills all over my body as I listened and watched attentively. I was spiritually salivated with a quest to indulge my finite appetite in a contemplation of the great deity of which the preacher spoke so eloquently about. I was fully satisfied with the service, knowing that nothing was going to hinder me from serving God. This was the moment of great truth concerning the god of the universe. The preacher pulled no punches; he expounded the Word of the scriptures with such authority, which left my humble soul in a penitent mode.

Although I had embraced the Christian faith prior to leaving home, I was not yet baptized, but was steadfast in the Word and the things pertaining to God. It was my desire to be baptized upon returning home the next school holidays, but now that I have found this new and wonderful fellowship in the Maida church, I was inclined to reconsider my previous decision making to become a member of my parents' church back home. However, I was caught in a serious plight, not knowing which direction to go on this very important religious matter. On the other hand, the fear of my parents' wrath was hanging over me if I contemplated the idea to join the old-fashioned Pentecostal church of God in Maida. I knew well that I would be adding fuel to the fire if I was to be baptized in my father's homeland without the permission of my parents, and I knew what the answer would be if I attempted to bring the subject to their attention. So I go on pondering in my spirit, seeking the good Lord's guidance on the path that I should take toward water baptism and church membership.

The next day, school began at Aboukir Educational and Industrial Institute; this was January 6, 1973. The cocks crowed early in the morning and woke me from sleep. For fear of being late on my first day of school, I was up and ready at five a.m. It was still dark outside and extremely cold. I waited patiently for the minibus that would take me to school that morning. It was a seven-and-a-half-mile journey from my house to the Aboukir school, and if I missed the minibus, I would have to walk that marathon to school on my first day. So I watched with eager eyes to see the light of that transport coming in the dark; and sure enough, it came and stopped at my feet, and I jumped up into the minibus and found out that it was standing room only on board.

It was ten minutes to six o'clock; the overloaded motor vehicle sped away with much urgency. The driver stopped several times on the road, picking up other students destined for the Aboukir Institute. I felt nervous, not knowing what to expect on the first day of school. A thousand thoughts flashed across my mind as the vehicle traveled at rapid speed over the rough unpaved roads of my father's homeland. There were times when I felt like my stomach was coming out of its place as the driver negotiated the dangerous corners of the parochial road. Thanks be to God! We finally reached the designated place of my disembarkation; the minibus stopped abruptly at the imaginary bus stop. My legs were cramped up, so I had to massage them back to normality before I could walk another feet up the steep hill to the school compound.

I looked with eagerness and in great anticipation, and then I finally saw the school. To my surprise, the building was not what I anticipated; it was a very old building, seemingly from the eighteenth century. There were brick walls, iron gates, roughly paved corridors, a nearby outdated-looking water tank, and a large pasture with a multitude of cows in the distance. My limbs dropped, and so did my spirit as I examined what would be my new institution of learning for the next three years. However, one thing that stood out on that campus that brought a ray of hope to my disappointed arrival was a brilliant painted sign that read Education Is the Key. It was then that I was reminded of the purpose for which I was sent to that faraway land. I was to take my stand and make my mark on the sands of time where great men and women have trod before, which includes my elder brother Errol, a graduate of that fine institution, who was now a fine policeman on his rounds.

I proceeded quickly to the school's auditorium with courage after reading the captivating motto of the Aboukir Institute. There was a vast student body present, which gave me an overview of the situation; everyone seemed elated to be at school as if this was a long dream come true for them. For me, it was the first nightmare of my higher education. The school activities began promptly under the capable leadership of the strict principal, Teacher Grant, who led the morning's devotional exercise and gave the official welcome to the students. Teacher Grant, as he was affectionately called, was a stern Baptist deacon from Lilly Field, one who had his cane outstretched, ready to administer lashes on the backs of those who might err. His opening speech drove fear in the new students' hearts that first day on campus. He categorically stated the rules of the institution in his opening stand and hastily introduced the penalties for breaking those rules. Teacher Grant's rigorous orientation lasted for one hour and fifteen minutes while the students sat and listened attentively. We were given handouts of the rules and regulations plus the school curriculum and were told to study and observe all the rules and regulations carefully. Discipline was the order of the day, and Teacher Grant made it a compulsory subject for all students. We had an early dismissal that first day, which gave us the opportunity to get acquainted with the facilities of the institution and with other students and teachers on campus. On tour we visited the food and nutrition department, industrial Art center, auto mechanic, auto electrician division, and the sports complex before leaving for home.

It was a fascinating day at school. I saw my future before me, and the thoughts of becoming a policeman like my brother Errol were foremost in my mind. It was then that I understood the reason for my brother's discipline; he had passed through the long arm of Teacher Grant's laws of self-discipline at the Aboukir Institute, and I was now a prime candidate for that unending process. I had no knowledge that I was already introduced to Teacher Grant School of Hard Knocks by my brother-in-law Keith over the summer holiday, so by the time I got to Aboukir Institute, my name was written in Teacher Grant's rigorous classroom of "the making of a student." Therefore, I was to conduct myself in a manner that will uphold the discipline and reputation of my brother.

Next day, classes began; it was time to settle down to some hard work. Devotion was compulsory for all students, commencing eight o'clock each morning in the main auditorium. After devotion, there was inspection parade. Teacher Grant would check out the students' socks, belts, shoes, and hair. He would normally run a pencil through the boys' hair to ensure it was properly combed. Any student found guilty of not combing their hair was immediately sent home on suspension. That student would have to bring a letter of apology upon returning to school; in addition, that student would have to stand before the entire school population and read the letter of apology aloud. No one could escape the discipline of Teacher Grant; he was rough and ready and feared no man that stood before him.

As the year progressed, I settled down to achieve the goals I set out to accomplish at Aboukir Institute. As the days went by, I soon found myself getting involved in various extracurricular activities including sports, student association, prayer cells, debating committee, etc. I soon became a prominent sportsman, a noted cricketer whose popularity spread across the campus in record time after having the glorious honor of bowling the famous West Indies cricket hero J. K. Holt Jr. for a duck in a cricket coaching expedition led by J. K. Holt Jr. and the famous West Indies spin bowler Alfred Valentine at Aboukir Institute Sports Complex. My name was written in the history book of time on that sunny afternoon of spring when I uprooted the wicket of one of the world's leading batsmen for a duck. I recalled this noble day at school, the day my fellow students crowned me hero of the match. But I knew it must have been some Providence that crossed my path and let me have the wicket of such illustrious stroke player in that glorious game of uncertainties.

I felt like a great fast bowler that day after I have taken the wicket of such a master of test cricket. Some of my fellow students thought I was a brilliant batsman, but it was that day that I was characterized as one of the most feared fast bowlers in the campus of Aboukir Institute. My older brother Errol, a former student of Aboukir Institute, had left his mark on the campus; so I had to live up to that standard. His name was imprinted in the minds of Teacher Grant, and oftentimes, he would implore me to follow the footsteps of my brother in striving hard for success. Therefore, I had to discipline myself in order to live up to the standard set by my brother.

The road to school was long and rocky; I was becoming restless and weary from traveling. My heart was set on home, wondering when I will return to see my family again. Memories of my leaving home came streaming down my mind as I yearned for the homeland of my birth. Despite the various attractions, friends, family, and fellowship, there was a void in me, a desire to be home with those I loved so dear. The beauty and glorious scenery of my father's homeland could not wash the memories of home from my mind. There were sleepless nights and twisted dreams in my dark midnights as the quest for my returning became stronger and stronger.

In all my struggles to get settled in that fair land of my father's birth, the blessed saints kept me anchored in Christ with many prayers and encouragements. The school taught me how to be a disciplined young man, which was the best preparation for all my tomorrows, and I could do nothing but surrender to the purpose for which I was sent to my father's homeland. I was conscious of the task that I was embarking upon the road I must trod in order to be successful in my educational pursuits. So I sacrificed the comfort of my hometown for the agony of my reluctant departure. It was the grace of God that kept me through the long midnights of my discomfort and led me to the quiet still waters of hope and joy as my spirit yearned toward the salubrious land of my birth.

By then, I had made up my mind that nothing could erase the memories of my birthplace, even if I cried a river of tears. So I went on, taking each day as it came, with a view to complete a seemingly unending journey to another side of life. I was conscious of the fact that life would not be this way for the rest of my days; I prayed earnestly that, that day will come when I will say my last goodbye to that distant land and journey back to the one I loved so dear. Until I rid myself of that present agony, there was no quick fix to my anguished soul. I had to tread the road to higher education and take with me whatever it brought, for this was the chartered course that was mapped out by my parents, and I could not contemplate another route.

The educational journey was destined for success, and I was given the charge to see it through no matter what it took or else face the challenge of the long arm of my father's law upon my returning home. So I had no choice in the matter. I had to pursue the task ahead with positive thoughts in order not to fall into a bitter remorse of unending sorrow, which could result in a tragic tale to be later told.

CHAPTER THREE
THE HOUR OF TOTAL RECONCILIATION

Subsequently, my Christian life was introduced to the most vigorous line of trials and endurance, which marked the true test of character. I needed to have a firmer grip on Christ in order to succeed as a student at the Aboukir Institute. The pressure was on from my peers who thought I was missing the fun of the world and the pleasure of sin. My schoolmates tried hard to get me on their side, which was the journey to the path of sin, but without success. Indeed, my faith at times wavered, and the fact that I was not yet baptized provided the option for me to stay in Christ or join the gang of sinners in their pursuit for wantonness. But the fear of God was upon me and would not let me go for nothing.

I was at a crossroad and must choose only one way, and I had to make that choice expeditiously. There was lots of idle jesting among my fellow students, especially those students whom I walked home with each day. There were many students who lived in Aboukir, so I had a great company of teenagers traveling with to and from school each day. Most of the boys had their girlfriends, and I had none, so I was seen as the odd boy in the group; the girls began to chase me with the intention to render me helpless to the will of the flesh. It was then that I knew I needed God's help more than any other time in order to keep my dignity and my soul from falling beneath the quicksand of immorality.

It was during those trying moments of my life that God proved Himself to me in an authentic manner. The youth department had planned a series of open-air meetings in the district of Lower Aboukir during the spring; it was at that time when I was procrastinating on the whole idea of continuing serving Christ as my personal savior. On the Thursday night of those meetings, God revealed Himself to me publicly during the meeting. The preacher made an altar call I did not respond to him because I knew I was already a Christian. He pointed his long finger at me and said, "Young man, I have a word from the Lord for you." I stood in awe as the fear of God suddenly gripped me. I stood there, trembling with fear and not knowing whether I should go to the preacher or stand my ground. When I did not respond immediately, he repeated his call for me to come to him. This time, I had no choice; every one's eyes were fixed on me as the anointed man of God spoke to me repeatedly. I walked slowly toward him with my head hanging down. He pointed his finger in my face and said, "Thus, said the Lord, I have called you and ordained you to be a pastor when you were only seven years old. I have chosen you and place my hand upon you that you should proclaim my Word to your generation." Immediately, the power of God came upon me, and I was overshadowed by the Holy Spirit. I felt like someone had a hold on me and would not let me go. The Holy Ghost-filled mothers of the church got a firm hold on me that night and began to pray with their hands fixed on my head. I felt like a captive prisoner in the hands of the prayer warriors. It seemed like their prayers were endless, but I could not escape from the grip of those strong women of God who held me captive until I fully surrendered to the will of God. It was then that I knew without any reservation that I had to remain in the pathway of Christianity.

The following Sunday morning, I went to church very early. Sunday school was about to begin, and the late Deacon Gray was serving as superintendent of the Sunday school department. After the fascinating lecture ended, it was time for reviewing the lesson taught; we were asked to repeat the golden text, which was taken from Hebrews 13:5: "Let your conversation be without covetousness; and be content with such things as ye have: for he had said, I will never leave thee, nor forsake thee." The students had to know the Sunday school lessons, especially the golden text; otherwise, Deacon Gray would be on our case, like Matlock, the private investigator until we have fully grasped the teaching of the day's subject matter.

It was youth Sunday; the youths were in action, fully in charge of the day's activities. Worship service began after the Sunday school ended, precisely at 11:00 a.m.; then came the singing of choruses that I have never heard before, but they brought a sense of joy to me as I tried to learn the words. It was in these moments of worship preparation that the church came alive and was set ablaze with spiritual fire. Songs of praises and inspiration rang out, and God's power came with flaming spell. The choir sang beautifully, and the tithes and offering was received reverently in a ceremonial mode; then the preacher was introduced to the vast congregation. He took his stand with confidence. He was the host pastor, Rev. James Walden, an anointed servant of God called to preach to that part of the native land, the land of my father's birth. He came from another part of the country, but was sent by his superior to take up pastorate in that side of the vineyard. He was short, thick, burly, dark, and strong. He wore a smile that brought hope to those who met him.

I could feel a chill running down my spine as he began to read the text from Ecclesiastes 12:1: "Remember now the Creator in the days of thy youth, while the evil days come not, nor the years draw nigh, when thou shalt say, I have no pleasure in them." The subject of his sermon was "Young man, I call upon you because you are strong." When he began to expound the Word of God, the Spirit was upon him, and he preached like fire was in his bosom. It seemed like God was talking directly to me through the preacher during his discourse. I felt the Spirit coming upon me like a convincing judge, speaking to my intellect. I was in a state of conviction. I knew something was going to happen that day that would probably change my life forever.

The hand of the Lord was upon me and carried me out in the Spirit from where I was sitting to the altar. I could not have held back the tears; it came rushing down my face. God's presence was there; it overshadowed me and left me with a broken heart and a contrite spirit. My life was totally lost in God, and I surrendered to His will. I cried a river, washing the memories of sin away. Calvary's cross became more meaningful to me; my hour had come, and I could not do anything but recommit my entire life to the saving knowledge of Jesus Christ, my redeemer. My night had surely passed; it was the breaking of a new dawn in my Christian life. I knew I was saved before leaving my homeland, but now the Holy Spirit gave me full assurance of salvation, and I was ready to tell the world that I was saved by His grace. There was a deep settled peace inside, a calm that I could not explain. The joy of the Lord had captured my entire being that day, and I was possessed with a divine compulsion mingled with godly fear. It was a brand-new feeling of heavenly excitement, which stunned my schoolmates who were present at church; they were left in awe and complete wonderment. The glory of God came upon me and renewed my spirit for Christian duties. "Therefore if any man be in Christ, he is a new creature: old things are passed away; behold, all things become new" (2 Corinthians 5:17).

Shortly after this encounter with God, the testing of my Christianity increased rapidly, but I knew the Lord was with me and that He was able to carry me through. So I held on firmly to God when temptations came. Not very long afterward, I was appointed to sing in the youth choir; in fact, I was the only male in the choir at the time, surrounded by a host of young ladies. At first, I felt a bit shy being placed in the company of so many women to sing in a vast choir; but as time went by, I got used to the fact that it was a privilege to be asked to serve in God's house. There was rapid growth in my youthful Christian life. I was eager to learn and had a passion for the souls of men; and as a result of that, I began preaching the Gospel of Jesus Christ, like a madman, all over town, leading others to the Lord Jesus Christ.

My theology was not necessarily in the proper order, but I had the anointing that propelled me to spread the word to all mankind. I held firmly to God as if salvation was running out of stock. The hand of the Lord was upon me. I could feel His presence near me in the land of Aboukir. The closer I got to God, the more my sinful nature was highlighted by the Holy Spirit, so I learned to rely upon Him only as my source of righteousness.

It was good to have touched the old-fashioned altar where sins are forgiven and crooked paths are made straight through the blood of Christ. Being reconciled to the Master in totality, I soon found out that I had new dreams and aspirations for the future and a desire to seek after God in a passionate way until all the fibers of myself were lost in the grandeurs of His beauty. The Holy Spirit was my road map on the pilgrim's journey for spiritual maturity in Christ Jesus, my Lord. All my sinful thoughts were surrendered to His will and lost in His infallible words. It had dawned upon me to seek after God and the things concerning Him with all my heart so that I might be saturated by His presence and His words always.

That moment of total reconciliation brought me to my bending knees in recognition of the supreme lordship of Jesus Christ. I became more and more engaged in the activities of the Maida church of God near the district of Aboukir, endeavoring to find God's perfect will for my life. And at the same time, I was wondering what my parents would say if I should be baptized in the Garden Parish of St. Ann in the old-fashioned church of God, as it was called by the skeptics of those days. There were surmounting fears and anxiety in my life as I sought to determine the destiny of my own life and the salvation of my soul with the guaranteed wrath of my father in the forefront of my confused thoughts.

My mind was at a two-way crossing, not knowing which road to take because my parents were anxiously waiting the day when I would return home to be baptized in their church, the Love Lane Church of God in my hometown. As for me, I was bent on becoming a member of the Maida New Testament Church of God; but the fear of disobeying my parents had a strong hold on me, and the expected consequences of my action was of course the major subject on my mind. So I temporary removed the baptismal thoughts from the shelf of my mind. However, I pressed on in Christ, keeping the faith, spreading gentleness wherever I went. I labored in various departments of the church until I forget that I was not yet baptized and received into the fellowship of the Maida New Testament church of God. So compulsive was my passion for souls that church membership became obsolete in my quest for spirituality.

Rev. James Walden, the then pastor, spoke to me on several occasions in regard to my water baptism and told me I could be baptized in the church at Maida; and he would later send a letter of commendation to my hometown pastor, Rev. R. C. McNally, for him to receive me into the membership of the Love Lane Church. The greatest fear in me was one word "disobedience." I dreaded it more than a soldier's rifle. As a child, I had known the Holy Scriptures and felt if I broke the laws of my parents' teachings, God would punish me. I feared the scripture that says, "Children, obey your parents in the Lord: for this is right. Honor thy father and mother; which is the first commandment with promise" (Ephesians 6:1-2).

I continued steadfast in the faith, serving Christ to the best of my ability, looking forward to my water baptism. It was a time of total recovery from my early childhood life of reckless behavior; my eyes were set on the heavenly portals of glory as the scriptures became my spiritual food for sustenance in the daily walk of life. I pressed toward the mark of holiness, despite the testing of my faith, seeking God's help in my time of severe trials.

In light of my total reconciliation to the Lord, I became more and more zealous and committed to the kingdom of God. The temptations and struggles of the Christian walk became more severe as the yearning for more of God manifested in my converted heart. News soon reached my homeland concerning the progressive growth in my Christian life in the Garden Parish of St. Ann. Prayers were constantly offered in my behalf by my parents and sisters back home, who were also of the household of faith and members of the Baptist church and the Love Lane Church of God respectively. These churches were in direct contrast to the old-fashioned New Testament Church of God where I was totally reconciled to God; but it was that noisy, hand-clapping, feet-stamping, tongue-talking, hallelujah-shouting body of believers that drove my soul toward a permanent status in Christianity. Now I am forever grateful for that monumental experience that has shaped my eternal destiny.

My quest for more knowledge of God and the church was almost fanatical as I sought every opportunity to know God in every sense of his divinity. This sometimes upset my relatives with whom I was living and my close friends, to the point where they thought I was too deeply entrenched in the subject of Pentecostalism. Subsequently, I was referred to as a religious fanatic because I indulged in the true meaning of worship, "in spirit and in truth." But in all of these direct attacks on my personal life, the desire to claim a place in the kingdom of God was unwavering in my mind. My thoughts were drowned in the infinite one, my spirit was preoccupied by the spiritual things of the kingdom of God, and my eyes were affixed to the cross of Calvary, a reconciled life addicted to the cause of the Christ and his church.

The teachers and students at my school could not comprehend the sudden altitude of spiritual gravity to which my life had ascended in such a short period of time, so they scoffed in ignorance at my compulsion to church attendance. I was steadfast in faith, not wanting any detour from what was right to what was wrong. The unselfish hand of the Almighty guided me to safe paths each time it seemed that I would stumble to places that were dark and contrary to the will of God. The things I used to do, I did them no more; it was church and God alone and most people thought that I had lost my mind because of my addiction to religious matters. To them, I was a handsome young lad, ready to fit in a vacant space in Satan's employment; but to their disappointment, I had gone to the "clapping hands church." "What a lost!" most people thought privately; others proclaimed it loud in my hearing. But I would have none of it, for I was reconciled to God for good, never to look back in this world of sin. After my total reconciliation to God in that blessed hour of repentance, it was no turning back for me.

Indeed, it was the turning point in my life that marked the mountain tracks for my future achievements, both sacred and secular. It was then that life became more meaningful and people became important, rather than mere existing matters upon planet Earth. The right path that I chose taught me the wrong that I had done and pointed me to the god of justification, who cleared my sinful account that was spiritually over drafted for many years. However, being reconciled did not guarantee me a trouble-free, easy pass through life's passage in a troubled world. In fact, there were times when I came close to the gates of hell on my pilgrim's journey but was always rescued by divine intervention in the death-crossing streams of my early Christian struggles.

So I pressed forward with God's protection over boisterous waves on tempestuous seas, with God in my heart, reconciling the world unto Him; and my face set like flint toward the New Jerusalem. I was driven by a passion that held me captive and would not release me for nothing, not even for a countless ransom. I was reconciled to God, and I truly understood the call to the Christian life of total commitment. And therefore, all to Jesus I surrendered and helplessly gave up my personal preference for the will of the Creator that I might be a prospective candidate for His employment in the fields of total reconciliation. My life was transformed by God the father, justified by Jesus Christ the Savior, and sanctified by the Holy Spirit.

The magistrate of heaven dropped my charges of reckless endangerment, illegal possession of destructive behavior, self-attained righteousness, and inherited religious eternal security. It was then that I fully grasped the understanding that my mother's Christianity could not guarantee me a place in the kingdom of heaven and that I needed my own personal encounter in God's courtroom before I could be properly vindicated.

Sure enough, that unforgettable hour came at the twilight of my teenage rampage when the god of all grace entered upon the castle of my heart and set up His eternal kingdom. I was submersed into His great ocean of love supplied by the streams of living waters, which flowed from the reservoir above.

I was totally reconciled for the Master's use and was fully aware of my indebtedness to the god of my salvation, cognizant of the fact that "to whom much is given, much is required." I went on my way, rejoicing in the fact that God forgave me of my low estate of sin and enabled and considered me to be a candidate for His eternal kingdom. This brought springs in my steps and tears in my eyes, knowing that a king has stooped so low to bring me to higher plains to the place where my sins were to be all washed away. I went on singing His high praises, acknowledging Him as the only true king of mankind, the monarch of the universe who through His precious son Jesus Christ has reconciled me unto Himself.

**Standing at the front yard of the Battle Factory Church
In My early Christian days**

CHAPTER FOUR

THE COMFORTER HAS COME

The desire for the things of God were strongly impressed upon my mind, but more forcefully was my need for the infilling of the Holy Spirit. In those early days of church life, the young people were more dedicated to duty and were very conscious about the spiritual work and well-being of the church than secular vocations and personal achievements. For us, it was God first, and everything else came after. This symbolized the way of life for the saints of that particular era. As a result of that, I became an active worker in the church after meeting certain criterion set by our pastor, which was mandatory for all Christian workers. For instance, any person who wished to work in any position in the church must be baptized in the Holy Spirit with the initial evidence of speaking in tongues. These positions include deacons, choir members, chairman of any board, Sunday school teachers, to name a few.

Therefore, seeking for the infilling of the Holy Spirit was paramount in the lives of the believers and was taught as a vital subject for spiritual growth and upward mobility in the church of God. Although my earnest desire to serve the Lord and the church was evident in my daily living, I needed to go one step further in God—that is, to seek earnestly for the baptism of the Holy Spirit in my life. Coming from a more sophisticated orthodox church background such as the Baptist in my childhood days and, later on, the love lane church of God, it was a difficult task in my prideful mind to demote my intellectual assent to the lowly dirt floor church of the Maida's old-fashioned hand-clapping and tongue-speaking church. This became an ensuing struggle in my spiritual bosom as I sought for the most important item on the church agenda, the baptism of the Holy Spirit.

Holiness was the watchword of my early religious upbringing in the church I attended in the earlier days, accompanied by practicing a quiet disposition in worship. Therefore, I faced with the challenge of transforming my former piousness in worship at the Love Lane Church of God into the new spiritual outburst of Testament Church of God style of worship, including speaking in a heavenly language that no man could speak by himself unless directed by the Holy Spirit. We were told by the spiritual mentors of our day that this experience comes only when a believer has a constant yearning, hunger, and thirst for the Holy Spirit. I told myself I would have none of this tongue-talking stuff. I was being driven by my own holy quietness and pride, struggling with the idea of a Holy Spirit baptism, and to add to my saga was the fact that I was to seek for the baptism of the Spirit in a public place in the company of my colleague. For me, this whole idea of worshipping in an unorthodox manner would have ruined my societal standing in light of my early religious upbringing. Most of my peers in the church were rooted in the soil of Pentecostalism; they were like fanatics without fear, and they were not afraid to make their belief and practice known to all the onlookers who heard them speak in tongues. I was adamant in my belief, not wanting to ruin the long-preserved reputation of my family heritage.

As a young Christian with a quest for knowledge, I was at a cross-road between my parents' church and my newfound church, the Maida New Testament Church of God in the Garden Parish. I was waiting for something to happen that would give me signals as to the direction that I was to take for my life regarding my water baptism and, subsequently, becoming a member of the Pentecostal movement before proceeding one step further in my decision making.

While continuing to seek more of the Lord, there was a thirst within me that could not be explained. The young people and older folks began to press upon me the importance of the Comforter, the Holy Spirit, in the life of a Christian. The baptism of the Holy Spirit was the main talk of the day; the believers constantly implored me to seek for the baptism of the Spirit and gave explanation as to the purpose and how one receives this baptism. The preachers of those days centered their sermons on the subject of the Holy Spirit baptism; this was also the main theme at prayer meetings and fasting services. In every corner of the church life, the Holy Spirit was highlighted, and people were encouraged to "get it and get it fast" because we were told by the elders that the baptism of the Holy Spirit was power for service and power to live free from sin.

As a sophisticated young man, I too soon was caught up in the powerful fever of that era and began to think and imagine about the wonders and great magnitude of this joy that was shared by those who had received the Holy Spirit baptism. I began to meditate deeply on the Word of God because even though I thought I had all the things that were needed to walk the walk of faith, I fell short of the most important one in my life—the baptism of the Holy Spirit, which was to transform my Christian life to a higher place and make the burdens of my sojourn lighter. The more they talked about the Comforter, the more I became thirsty, hungry, and anxious to receive from God this promise. I began to search the scriptures diligently on matters of the Holy Spirit, and it was then that I came face-to-face with God through the inspired Word of God in the Acts of the Apostles: "But ye shall receive power, after that the Holy Ghost is come upon you: and ye shall be witnesses unto me both in Jerusalem, and in all Judea, and in Samaria, and unto the uttermost part of the earth" (Acts 1:8).

This was a promise given to the disciples by Jesus. After reading this word, I knew I had to change my philosophy of worship and get ready for a new dimension in God. It was time for a change; being humbled by the Word of God, I came down from my lofty height of self-pride to embrace the way of Pentecostalism. However, the transition was not an easy one because it brought me some pains, some trials, and then some tears. In those days, the folks lived as though Jesus was coming back from heaven the next day to take them home. They did not want to miss the rapture of the church and certainly not to lose out on the chance to receive the baptism in the Holy Spirit. The popular notion of the era was "the same things that prevent you from receiving the baptism of the Holy Spirit could prevent you from going up in the rapture." This popular saying brought a strong sense of urgency to the Body of Christ, and many were challenged by the elders to seek for such infilling with a sense of determination.

Some of the saints often told me, "You can't live without the Holy Spirit, my brother. You need to go on some fasting and prayer." These older Christians were serious as the Judges of the Old Testament. The elders did not accept any excuse from the members who were not filled with the Spirit. Those believers were sometimes told, "Perhaps you are not living right before God, and that could be the reason you are not filled with the Holy Spirit." It was out of concern for the well-being of the people that the elder spoke and not because they were more spiritual than the others. They were humble saints from the countryside; some were unlearned and had no formal education or theological understanding, but they were seers and discerners who often heard from God. Those who were accosted by the elders would go to God in remorse and repentance, begging Him to clear their records in order to qualify them for the Holy Spirit baptism rather than to get upset and be offended by such blatant accusations.

The fear of God was evident in the church; the daily password was "Are you filled with the Holy Spirit?" I had no choice but to join the crowd of seekers or be left alone as a conscientious objector in the grandstand of the critics watching the Pentecostal tongue-speaking bandwagon pass me by. My best choice was to join the holy throng of Protestants that was undoubtedly driven by a divine compulsion, which pushed them to the edge of their pride and caused them to be lost in the god of the Bible. I was instantly stripped of my own denominational orthodoxy when the Holy Spirit rented my contemplating heart, replaced my pride with a contrite spirit, and brought me to my bending knees in silence and tears.

I began to pray and fast like never before, mingled with a passion to claim that which was the promise of God, the Comforter, called the Holy Spirit. For many days, I could not eat. I replaced food with fasting, playing with prayer. Aunt Daughta, Keith's mom was a conservative Anglican and her coffee plantation became my altar of prayer. I went down to the plantation to pray daily so as not to disturb her and the other folks with whom I was living. My quest for the power of God was unwavering; the older folks gave me much encouragement in my daily pursuit of the Comforter. So I pressed on with godly excitement, being driven by the courage of others.

There was no time to idle; everyone was on the move for God, striving toward perfection in the Christian walk of life. The baptism in the Spirit was a vital necessity in the lives of the believers. There were times when I felt discouraged after much praying and fasting and did not receive the Holy Spirit, but the good old mothers of the church cheered me on, telling me the blessing was just around the corner. This gave me a sense of anticipation mixed with anxiety. The saints never ceased to comfort and encourage me along my journey to the Spirit-filled destination to which I was heading. They carefully guided me though the rigorous passage of Satan's domain and rebuked any sign of familiar spirit that would attempt to obstruct my passage to the ultimate goal.

It was on the first Sunday of March in the year 1976 when a great revival camp meeting began at Murray Mount in St. Ann, Jamaica, West Indies, where a new church was about to be born to the church of God district of churches in that area. This community was infested with notorious drug gangs. It was the well-known headquarter of the country's main marijuana production and gangs' head offices. But on that bright Sunday evening of March at seven o'clock, it was invaded by Holy Ghost-filled Pentecostal watchdogs from the tongue-talking church of God at Maida. It was a long and strenuous walk for most of the saints who lived in the districts of Maida and Aboukir, but they were determined to bring about change to the people of Murray Mount. The blood-washed saints did not waver nor shrink in the face of imminent threats from the gangs of the day; they turned their attention toward the god of deliverance, who could help them deliver Murray Mount from the chains of the devil.

My final exams were on, but I sacrificed some of my study time in order to attend the camp meetings and set aside one day of each week for fasting and prayer in my quest to receive the baptism of the Holy Spirit. We had to travel nine miles one way to the place where the meetings were held, most times on foot because transport was limited in those days. The road was rough and rocky; we walked over steep hills and mountainous terrains each night where the stars were the only light to guide us through dangerous paths in the absence of streetlights in that remote part of the island. The road was sometimes dark and dismal when the dark clouds hid the moon away from us. With much faith, spiritual courage, and great endurance, the journey seemed lighter to the traveling band of Christian soldiers destined for success. There was much singing in the dark each night en route to Murray Mount, which indicated to the gang members that an army of God's people was on a mission, and they were to put up their guns and other weapons because we were only passing through and needed a clear passage to the meetings.

Each evening, as planned, I would give Sister Blossom, the youth director, a shout when reaching her house a few blocks from my house in the district of Aboukir. Although the road was long, rocky, and dangerous, Sister Blossom would gather all the young people each evening for the trip to Murray Mount; she was an outstanding dedicated leader and companion in the Gospel for the cause of the young people of the church of God. The road to Murray Mount was similar to the road that led from Jerusalem to Jericho in biblical times, noted for thieves and vagabonds. We were sometimes afraid to attend the meetings when we learned of gang warfare and killing on a given night, but as young people, we decided that we would not allow the devil to extinguish our spiritual fire nor detour our quest for the baptism of the Holy Spirit. We planned a strategy to walk and talk in groups, watching one another's backs in order to escape ambush in the dark.

There was a well-known gang consisting of eleven men who prowled our traveling route to Murray Mount each night. They were on the police's most wanted list; these men had no fear for God or men. They were armed and dangerous, men who had committed the most hostile crimes against humanity; they have created absolute pandemonium upon the citizens of the community. Added to our dilemma was the declaration of the state of emergency by the then government across the entire country. The military were called out of camp to help the police crush the upsurge of political and gang violence. We too as young people were called out for battle, to take up the weapons of our warfare—our M66, the Bible rightly divided, of prayer, fasting, and the anointed Gospel preaching. Now I knew that I needed that coveted tool, the Holy Spirit, which is called "the dangerous weapon in the hand of a righteous man." I began to seek God more earnestly with a view to overcome all fears of the enemy and to be equipped with the Holy Spirit, which had brought courage to those among us who were filled with the baptism of the Holy Spirit.

In the midst of these turbulences, the camp meetings proceeded in high gear at Murray Mount. Many nights while traveling in the darkness to church, we were pranced upon by squads of soldiers on patrol on the route to the meetings. These armed members of the security forces were out looking for wanted men in the area, and they stopped and searched everyone who passed that way. Nevertheless, we hastened to the house of God without fear, knowing that the good Lord would be with us. It was then that I felt the greatest zeal for the power of the Holy Spirit in my life. I made a covenant with God that first week of the camp meeting that I would not let the meeting end without receiving the baptism of the Holy Spirit in my life. This was my resolution, and I was determined to let it happen no later than then.

The presence of God was literally evident in the meeting the first week; dozens of people received the baptism of the Holy Spirit, and a host of sinners came to know the Lord Jesus as their personal savior. Hundreds of people of all walks of life emerged upon the consecrated ground at Murray Mount to lift up the name of Christ, their king.

In the second and third weeks of the meetings, the spirit moved upon the believers like flaming spells of fire from God's fireplace, which burned out sin and set the saints on spiritual fire. The entire community of Murray Mount was disturbed by a divine intervention in the little dirt-floored, coconut-branch-roofed church at the side of the road. Evangelist J. H. Higgins proclaimed the Word of God without fear or favor in the midst of principalities and demonic powers. The anointed preacher man sounded the alarm in the holy mountain of God despite the overcast clouds of marijuana smoke from the cliff of the drug dons, who perched on the church window in lawless behavior.

The church had been the subject of various persecutions at the time of the Gospel camp meeting. The building was previously set on fire during the outburst of political violence and was in the rebuilding process. Based upon my experience, the Holy Spirit always intervenes most powerfully in the affairs of humanity when the church was at her highest point of persecution. The Spirit came like violent winds from tempestuous seas and brought a perfect calm to man's untold sorrow and peace of mind in the time of great conflicts. Subsequently, the drug dons were overtaken by the intervention of the Holy Spirit, and some of them were seen laying flat on the red dirt floor of the Church. They were literally slain by the Holy Spirit, as they surrendered their lives to the will of God.

In this meeting, I saw a great chance to cash in on this amazing gift of the Holy Spirit as the final week of the camp meeting drew near to its close. Many of the saints who came to the meetings received the Holy Spirit baptism and went away rejoicing night after night. I watched each night as the folks were slain in the Holy Spirit and rendered frantically spiritually paralyzed on the red dirt floor, speaking in other tongues that were not of man but from God. A suppressed pride raised its ugly head within me, telling me, "You must not hit the turf, or else your peers will laugh at you." For a while, my thoughts began to wonder from the church to places here and there; my concentration was out of range, and I was losing altitude from the covenant I made with God. The fact that the floor of the little church was covered with strong red dirt, I was deeply concerned about falling on the floor. I knew my time was running out and faster than I thought because the campaign was coming to a close, and I had not yet received the baptism in the Holy Spirit.

It was Friday night, March 28, 1976, the final night at Murray Mount when it seemed like the floodgates of heavens were opened. God's Spirit moved upon the preacher like never before in those meetings. It felt like God had come to earth in person that night. There was a spiritual vibration in church that shook the foundation of hell and brought sinful marijuana smokers to their bending knees at the altar before the preacher concluded his sermon. The church was in a militant mode as the preacher gave the altar call. Scores of men and women responded to the invitation to salvation. The altar was filled with penitent people weeping and asking for God's forgiveness. The saints were in constant fervent prayer, the congregation was charged with the Spirit of God, and many saints received the baptism of the Holy Spirit sitting in their pews.

Suddenly, the preacher shouted, "All those who need the Comforter, come forward to the altar. The Spirit is waiting!" Without hesitation, I rushed to the altar, knelt down, and started praying, pouring out my heart to the Lord. The hand of the Lord was upon me while I was at the altar and carried me out in the realms of the spirit in His supernatural power. By this time, I had forgotten about the dirt floor and my friends and those who were around me. I was taken out of my selfish self to a godly height. I had a clear vision that *I was flying away in the sky*. I could hear singing in the background like that of angelic hosts. The song was one I knew. "By and by, when the morning comes, when all the saints of God are gathered home." In the vision, I saw a wooden cross in an upright position, with streams of blood flowing down from the top, and then I saw Jesus coming out of the clouds with a golden crown in his hands. I heard a loud voice saying, "I'll give you this crown to wear if you take up that cross." The crown came closer to my head; there was a cool breeze blowing across the sky where I was. I rushed to the cross hugged it firmly, Then suddenly, the golden crown fell on my head, and I began to speak in unknown tongues as the Spirit gave utterance.

There was an outburst of praise all over the congregation when I spoke in unknown tongues. I felt like a wildfire in my bosom when the Holy Spirit came upon me that Friday night. I felt intoxicated; my entire being was captivated by the Holy Spirit, and I was set ablaze by a spiritual fire. I knew then that the Comforter has come. His presence was evident upon me, and my self-will was utterly destroyed by the will of God. The Spirit swept through the church like a mighty hurricane, leaving thirsty Christians saturated by the flood of God's power. I was completely captivated by the power of God, and I felt a stream of divine blessings flowing into my being. It was a night of heaven on earth; I could not stop praising God for answering my prayer. I continued rejoicing in the god of my salvation; the glory of God had arisen upon me in a forceful way and transformed my stubborn will for the glory of His name. Heaven kissed earth that Friday night in Murray Mount; my night was turned to day, and my burdens rolled away. It was an historic night—not only for me, but for all those who came to the meeting on that final night of heavenly glory at Murray Mount church of God. The attendees to the camp meeting came from all over; they came from as far as Aboukir, Cave Valley, Flat Rock, and McKenzie. The final night was the most attended, the same night I received the Comforter. Revival broke out in Murray Mount like a river taking back its course by forceful advance. I could not have held my peace; there was a fire shot up in me that could not be explained by finite man. There was shouting on the hill of Murray Mount. I felt so strong, renewed, and empowered by the divine; and no one could contain me. My outburst was at times boisterous, yet glorious as I journeyed home from church. The Comforter came on time; my prayers were answered. God came on time to where I was and revealed Himself to me in no uncertain terms, and I knew it was the beginning of a new day in my Christian life.

My entire being was possessed by the Holy Spirit when the flaming spell of the Spirit came upon me down at the altar. It was the fulfillment of my long yearning for the baptism in the Spirit. The saints rejoiced with me in that victorious moment of heavenly intervention. Like Isaiah, "mine eyes had seen the King, high and lifted up." The hills of Murray Mount lit up with the glory of God, and the people shouted with a crescendo of praise from the deep part of their hearts. We saw the hand of God at work in a personal way, and we were changed forever.

For me, it was a moment that I thought heaven had kissed earth in unison. The experience was too dramatic to forget, too real to have doubted, and too rapturous to have kept it selfish; so I went on my way, telling the good news that the Comforter had come. It was a flight into the grandeurs of the supernatural, which knocked out my human estate and left me floating in a divine altitude of the vast spiritual bliss of heaven. The Spirit was in me, and I was totally controlled by Him, who held me like a captive combatant for His sacred purpose. I heard singing in my spiritual ears; it was the glorious voices of an unknown choir singing this song:

O spread the tidings 'round,
Wherever man is found,
Wherever human hearts and
Human woes abound;
Let ev'ry Christian tongue
Proclaim the joyful sound:
The Comforter has come!

The Comforter has come,
The Comforter has come!
The Holy Ghost from heav'n
The Father's promise giv'n,
O spread the tidings 'round,
Wherever man is found—
The Comforter has come!

Evidently, the Comforter came for me that last night of the camp meetings in Murray Mount. It came *like a rushing mighty wind*; it came upon my parched soul and endued me with heavenly power from God's highest glory. I felt like my entire being was electrocuted by a high-power voltage, which rendered me almost speechless, propelling me to do extraordinary things. It was an unforgettable night that was recorded in the spiritual archives of the Christian church. Until my glorious tale is told at home or across the rolling tides, my heart will go on singing about that night when I saw the glory of God on earth. I never cease to testify of God's goodness again and again, and someday I'll sing with the choir of angels above "The Comforter Has Come."

The contemplation on my water baptism had by now began to manifest once again in my mind with extreme pressure. My mental faculty was becoming overburdened with the stress of decision making. Mom and others had received the news from the Garden Parish that I was inching closer and closer to Pentecostalism, retrieving from the old tradition they had brought me up in since my childhood days. I knew the traditional church had eyes on me regarding becoming a member and subsequently taking up an active and pivotal role in the congregation at Love Lane upon my returning home. However, my mind was preoccupied with the Pentecostal way of worship and, in particular, the New Testament Church of God at Maida. Therefore, I was lurking between two denominational columns without any settled baptismal arrangement beneath my religious feet. In spite of this hindrance, my life became a vehicle for the heralding of the Gospel of salvation to the lost. Soon after it was noised abroad that I received the baptism of the Holy Spirit at Murray Mount, doors began to open for me to preach the Word of God in various communities and churches.

I capitalized on the opportunity given to me to proclaim the Word of God; however, many folks thought I was going crazy, the way I talked about the work of the Lord. Some even dubbed me as the "church fanatic." At the pace I was going, many people thought that rapture of the church was nearer than ever before. My own relatives whom I lived with at Maida thought something had gone wrong with my brain, but it was the Comforter within my converted bosom that propelled me to do the things I did. Those who truly knew me knew that I was not an emotional person; but ever since that night when I received the baptism of the Holy Spirit, my life had taken a U-turn, and there was no stopping in my proclamation of the Gospel of Jesus Christ.

I could not have kept back the message of salvation that was coming from my concerned soul, so I heralded it loud and clear throughout the community. And when they inquired of the reason for my sudden boldness, they were told, "The Holy Spirit came upon him at Murray Mount." I continued to preach the Word of the Lord far and near, sharing the testimony of the outpouring of the Holy Spirit on my life wherever I traveled. At school, it was noted that something had happened to me. I was acting differently than before. I was not afraid to publish my newfound experience among the lecturers and students because the joy was overwhelming within me. Many of my schoolmates were Christians but did not believe in the baptism of the Holy Spirit; they thought that the tongue-talking churches were too old-fashioned for modern times, but I let them know the Holy Spirit was for all seasons. The educated critics at school did not leave me comfortless in their quest to dislodge me of my spirituality. But the heavenly Spirit was too forceful in me and I was not shaken by human ideologies. It was the manifestation of the Holy Spirit in my live that puzzled the minds of my intellectual onlookers. How the Spirit made me run, jump, and shout were part of the amazing saga in my quiet disposition that could not be understood by my opponents. There were constant persecutions from a gang of lawbreakers in the community, determined to render me helpless in the walk of my Christianity. These men were on the police's most wanted list. They were fierce and fearless, ruff and rugged; they roamed the streets of Maida, seeking for preys to devour. They had guns that would scare any man. I too had mine, only that it was legal: my M66, the Bible—the type that makes sinners tremble and backsliders repent. I was armed and dangerous, being occupied with the newfound experience of the Holy Spirit outpouring upon my life. The testing of my faith became more severe, but the weapon of my warfare was not natural; it was spiritual, it was my M66 (my bible) and I put it on rapid expressions in times of confrontation.

There were times when my life was in danger, threatened by the unruly wanted men who prowled the streets at night. My aim was steadfast, and my mind was made up; and if I should die, I was willing to do so for the cause of the Gospel. As a young man, I was intent on making Christ known to my fellow students and even those that were a threat to the security of the community. I often confronted then with the Gospel when I had the opportunity to converse with them, and to the most part, they would listen to me and requested prayer.

The coming of the Holy Spirit in my life created a vast difference. I was totally transformed and had a different outlook on life and everything that moved around me. I was on the cutting edge of a spiritual explosion when the Comforter came and brought order in my chaos and turned my thirsty soul into a stream of living water. Then I went on, bound by the Spirit, spreading the good tiding around wherever men were found. The long, long night had passed; the day came at last, and my vision was clear as I journeyed toward my eternal destiny. The spiritual fogs of doubt vanished from my mental sky when the Spirit came rushing down my way.

Onward with the Lord I traveled, driven by the Holy Spirit and set ablaze with spiritual fire. My head upright, my feet shod, my sword sharpened and dipped in the blood of Jesus Christ, and my face turned toward the New Jerusalem, I was confident that the end was near; I had the Comforter and had no fear. Thank God Almighty, the Comforter had come, and the Holy Ghost was given. My heart rejoiced, and my spirit magnified the great God of my father who had lavished me with the gift of His Holy Spirit.

CHAPTER FIVE

BURDENS ON MY JOURNEY: PART ONE

In the great height of my spiritual fulfillment, God was preparing me for future adversity unknown to me. After receiving the baptism of the Holy Ghost, the pressure and tension became more and more unbearable in my father's homeland. Due to my Pentecostal outburst, I was becoming a real threat to peace and quietness in the more traditional orthodox home of my kinfolks. This, of course, brought much discrepancy in our religious deliberations and discontentment over my Pentecostal manifestation. My life was sandwiched between the Anglican rites and rituals of my kinfolks and the tongues-speaking church that I embraced. There were disagreements and discontentment in the home due to my outspoken Pentecostal discourses both at church and home. I was experiencing the bonds of afflictions, which brought much burden on my pilgrim's journey.

My Christian life was severely tested and I was at an acute angle as I was contemplating to return home. During this time, my parents received word that I was getting out of hand, in their context, based on the report they received from my kinfolks whom I was living with at the time on that side of the island. Knowing my parents very well, I knew I was up for a rough landing in my native village of Spring Bank. As the Pentecostal flame burned within me, my heart yearned for home with mixed expectations. There was an intense battle within me as I wrestled with the serious decision making—whether to remain at Aboulkir and complete my education, or to return to my homeland to face the long arm of my father's law.

One Sunday afternoon while I was walking home from the church at Maida, the Spirit of the Lord spoke to me clearly, and it was then that I understood that the Lord was giving me the marching order to leave my father's homeland. It was getting more and more uncomfortable living with my kinfolks, and to add to that, the long seven-mile journey to school, sometimes on foot, was becoming unbearable. I thought of my homeland, my parents, brothers, sisters, and friends at home enjoying the cool breeze of the Blue Mountain and the beautiful white-sand beaches. Instead, I was far away in a strange village that had become my home for almost three years. The memories of home kept flashing down the corridors of my mind and brought tears to my eyes. The land of my father was beautiful, mountainous, and green, with lush vegetations; but I had another land in view. It was the land of my birth where the breeze was always blowing, and the sky seemed to touch the earth. A bundle of joy was in my heart as I yearned for the day of my departure.

It was nearing summer holiday, and I knew the end was near for me to bid the last farewell to that fair land. Finally, I mustered some courage and notified Aunt Daughta, my kinfolks, the church, and my schoolmates of my plans to depart the village of Aboukir and the church at Maida. It was a sad moment when I broke the sudden news, which was met with surprise, sadness, and tears. The youths were brokenhearted when they learned that I was leaving for good; as a result of this, they congregated each night after service to have the final moments of fellowship with me. The days were counting down rapidly, and many hearts were aching within the camp of the believers, including mine. The church folks were extremely supportive, kind, and affectionate as always, deeply connected to me in so many ways; and there was a common thread of love in our community circle. There were moments of sadness and strong crying as I recalled the day of my arrival in my father's land; and even though I was reluctant in going there, I grew to love that place like it was my own, but now it was time to go back to the place called home.

As it began to draw near toward the last day of June 1976 there was a sad feeling inside of me that I never felt before. It was the last day of the spring semester. I ventured upon one of the worst tasks of my youthful days to bid farewell to all my teachers and schoolmates at the Aboukir Institute. To many of them, this was a great surprise to learn that I was about to depart from that community. My departure was not announced at school, so many of the students had no knowledge that I was leaving town. When the news was noised around the campus, students from all walks of life came and hugged me; some kissed me while others shook my hand and walked away sadly. That final school day at Aboukir was a heartbreaking one, filled with sad parting and tears; this was the last time my feet had touched the green grass of the Aboukir Institute. I left the campus with a broken spirit and a sorrowful heart. My task was unfinished; my course was uncharted. I had not fulfilled my dreams to graduate from that prestigious institution of learning. I was on the cutting edge of a bright tomorrow, with a fixed scenario to walk in the footprints of my elder brother Errol all the way to Port Royal Police Academy; but instead, my eyes were turned from that bright sunshine of that horizon and detoured by some unknown force to the paths that I did not intend to venture upon until I have finished my course and achieved my coveted goals.

Then came the sad day of my last farewell, the day my relatives and friends planned to bid me Godspeed from their land to mine. It was the twilight of July 3, 1976. They came from near and far; there was sadness in their tear-filled eyes. Old and young people, schoolmates and young men and women from all over gathered at my farewell service at Maida New Testament Church of God to say goodbye to a simple country boy who had touched their lives one way or another. Sister Blossom, the youth director, gave a moving speech, which left tears in my eyes. She was followed by Sister Maxine Brown; and then came Brother Sam, Brother Harris, and Brother Profit with his musical piece. Everyone gave their expressions and made known their disappointment concerning my abrupt departure. When the time for prayer came, I was escorted to the old-fashioned altar by the elderly Deacon Gray, my Sunday school teacher. The pastor, Rev. James Walden, and others joined in prayer in my behalf. They laid hands upon me as customary and summoned heaven for more than one hour in concert prayer, seeking God's protection and guidance upon my young life.

I felt the presence of the Holy Spirit and the love of the people of Maida and Aboukir. When the moving service ended, dozens of young people swarmed me like bees, hugging and kissing me, sobbing, and crying; occasionally, some loud outburst could be heard in the distance as the people pressed upon me to get a last goodbye kiss, a hug, or a handshake. A great number of the young people walked me home that night, comforting and encouraging me the last mile of the way. Some of them sat up with me for most of the night, talking about the good old days of the past. Others tried to persuade me to stay in my father's homeland, but my mind was already fixed on returning home. One of my closest friends, Toney (Ratta) Keith's Nephew, who lived in the same house where I was living, could not accept the fact that my time was at hand. He recalled the days when we would go bird shooting, rabbit chasing, and orange picking on Mass Ira, my uncle's farm down at Maida Road. You could tell that Ratta had lost his best friend, the way he spoke that night, with tears in his eyes. He was only fourteen years old; he saw me as his hero, but now I was leaving, and it broke his heart deeply. So I promised him faithfully to write as often as I could and visit when I could. I knew the distance seemed endless, like a land across the sea, so it could be a very long time before we would see each other again. In those days, a farewell service could be compared to a funeral service because of the sorrow and sadness that it entailed. It felt like we were not going to see our loved ones again. This was a heartbreaking experience for me, so my hopes and dreams were to now center on the thought that I would never get attached to so many people again.

Next day was Monday, the fourth of July; it was time to leave the communities of Aboukir and Maida for good. The early-morning dew sent chills on my brow; the singing of birds in the nearby coffee plantations echoed their sweet voices of melody across the quiet community of Aboukir. Outside the gate were a few kindred folks who came to see me off. It was six o'clock in the morning when the transport came, a minivan, bound for the metropolitan city of Brown's Town. I bid farewell to Ratta, Grandpa, Grandma, Aunt Daisy, and Cheryl before hopping into the colorful minivan driven by Keith. Soon, the bus sped away from the scene, leaving behind Ratta's hand stuck in the air with a final goodbye gesture. I looked back from where I was sitting, and he was still standing there in disbelief; his best friend and partner was gone. I felt the pain of leaving my loved ones behind. I cried uncontrollably, trying to wash the memories of my short but interesting life in Aboukir away.

Upon reaching Brown's Town, I had to transfer to another minivan destined for Runaway Bay in order to catch the big Honey Bee bus for the final trip to my hometown, which was about one hundred and twenty-one miles away. As usual, the Honey Bee bus reached Runaway Bay at eight o'clock each morning on its journey from St. James to Portland. Luckily, one seat was vacant, and the conductor said, "Man, you lucky fi true, sih wan seat de." I was glad for the seat because the journey ahead was very long and tiresome. The driver was tall and lanky and had no tendency for hospitality. He knew the art of driving, and no one could negotiate the dangerous corner better than him; he was nicknamed Shots, perhaps because of the speed to which he drove the bus or the frequency of his stops at the bars along the way and the rapidity of his drinking. If you think you could dictate to the driver concerning his driving, you would be up for a rude awakening. He was the man in charge of your life for the next four hours of hell on earth, and you had better get used to prayer when the over-proof Jamaican white rum kicked into his ignorant head at ninety miles per hour on the rough potholed road across the north coast of the island.

As for me, previous experiences on the Honey Bee bus allowed me to understand the value of prayer. Generally speaking, the drivers oftentimes stopped at most of the bars, stopped at all his baby mother's house for twenty minutes or so, and even parked by a roadside restaurant to eat while the passengers sat restless and dissatisfied. But I had no other choice; if I missed that bus, my chances of reaching home would be very dim. The bus was now en route to Portland, stopping for anyone at any point; it seemed like it was going backward at times because of the many stops along the way. I knew well that I must consult God for journeying mercies if I was to get home safely. So at forty miles per hour, I prayed, "Guide me, O thou great Jehovah." At fifty miles an hour, I prayed, "Jesus, keep me near the cross." At sixty miles per hour, I prayed, "Nearer, my God, to Thee." At seventy miles per hour, I started singing, "All to Jesus, I surrender." And at ninety miles per hour, I prayed, "Lord, I am coming home."

The driver navigated the overloaded bus around the dangerous corners; my mind began to travel down memory lane, much faster than the moving bus. I was caught between the past experiences of my father's homeland and the future expectations of my homecoming. My mental skies were foggy, and the dreams of a happy landing were shattered by the past experiences of my father's whip. So the journey became even more burdensome for me. I knew that all was not well with my parents and me prior to my departure from Aboukir. The major problem was religion. I had become a Pentecostal preacher, and this brought much trouble between my parents and me. My pilgrimage was surrounded with endless questions, which seemed to have no answers. My mind was on the scenes of my home and the expected reactions of my father for I know that my arrival was not going to be an easy one when my feet touched that homeland.

The final lap of my journey was closer; a thousand thoughts flashed across my mental sky as I pondered over what might await me at home. The encumbered journey was by now adding anxiety to my life, and I was sweating in the cool temperature of that salubrious part of the island. The memories of the past crack of my father's whip upon my back began to haunt me like a ghost in a dark room on a stormy night. I felt in my spirit that I was getting ready for a rude awaking at home. Notwithstanding the joy I was experiencing on the earlier part of the journey, I was now on the brink of a nightmare, with sorrow in my breast and anxiety in my heart.

When we came close to the border of the parish of Portland, you could feel a difference atmosphere; a fresh, unpolluted breeze blew into the fast-moving bus. It felt like the air condition was just switched on, but it was nature's way of welcoming a native son back to the glorious land of his ancestors. There came upon me increasing burdens on my journey as I pressed toward my homeland, not knowing what tomorrow would bring—sorrow, sunshine, or rain. It was my determination to press forward despite of the unexpected moments ahead. Therefore, I summoned the god of my father for renewed strength to face the coming days, and He assured me of His sufficient grace that was able to carry me through.

My next task was to prepare myself for whatever awaits me at home and to make myself believe that all would be well with my parents and me. This, no doubt, was the highlight of the first phase of burdens on my journey that would later mark out the track to various trials and persecutions on my young Christian life. There were mixed emotions within me as I inched closer to the beautiful home I once lived prior to my departure to the Garden Parish of St. Ann, my father's birthplace.

Home At Last

After traveling through approximately eleven major towns of the island, we finally arrived in Port Antonio, the capital city of Portland, located at the skirt of the Blue Mountain, overlooking the beautiful Caribbean ocean. The city was lavished with lush green grass and vegetations. The glorious sunset shone across the deep blue sea, creating a crystal glaze upon Bryan's Bay; the birds sung sweetly in the nearby tress, and the schoolchildren walked happily down the street from school. The large bus came to a final halt at the market square terminal. The weary passengers began to disembark slowly; some were suffering from cramps and fatigue due to the overloaded conditions on board. Some were fast asleep; others tried to straighten out their crushed clothes affected by the sardine-packed public transport. I too had my moment only that it was with God alone where I had a short prayer to Him, thanking Him for journeying mercies.

The evening was quiet and cool; the marketplace was empty. The night clouds were slowly gathering across the eastern sky. I began to walk down West Street, observing the city I left three years ago. There was constant excitement within me as I met old friends and relatives along the way home. Unfortunately for me, the journey had not yet ended; in fact, it was the commencement of another. I had to walk three and a half miles from the bus terminal to my home at Spring Bank. This phase of the journey was a very mountainous, coupled with unpaved roads and sharp curves. There were no streetlights, and very few motor vehicles passed by that route. Taxi service was minimal, and hardly any taxi driver would dare venture upon such atrocious roads, even if I had offered to double the fare.

My final strides began with a few weary steps down the road. It felt like a thousand miles away. The night was coming fast, faster than my swift glides on the dim-lighted streets of Bound Brook Road. A million thoughts flashed through my mind like the rushing tides of Hurricane Flora's blast. I needed to keep focus to face the enormous challenge ahead, that of coming face-to-face with my father's wrath. I was coming home like the prodigal son, not knowing what would befall me upon reaching there. Soon, the darkness came before I left the major towns; the smaller villages had no public streetlights. It was pitch-black, dark like a thousand midnights put together. I had neither flashlight nor a bottle torch to help me find my way home; there were no stars in the sky to guide my battered feet. I had to feel my way through the dark streets of Spring Bank Road if I must get to my final destination. The road was lonely and desolate, except for a few ghosts who patrolled that route on a regular basis. I whistled and sang hymns in order to drive fear away from me in the dark territories of Satan's domain. The god of comfort gave me peace in those dark hours of my midnight. In those lonely moments, the god of the universe put strength in my weary feet as I pressed toward the family home.

When I finally reached home, it was after eight p.m. The house was filled with joy and added excitement. Greetings and salutation began to pour out, first from my parents, then from my brothers and sisters. It felt like a grand reunion; we hugged, kissed, and rejoiced together. My heart was flowing with joy as a result of the welcomed reception I received on arrival.

We then had dinner together around the huge dining table. For me, it was a dream comes true. I was home at last, not on holidays as usual, but I was home for good. Although tired and weary, my sisters and I still found time to chat for a few hours before retiring to bed. Our bedtime was usually ten o'clock in the evening, and for the girls, nine p.m. This was a part of my father's rules and regulations, and they were to be kept without wavering. As a result of my homecoming, the time was suspended for that night so that we could catch up on old time's stories. After a while, my father would walk through each bedroom and say, "All lights out, masters." It was then that we knew that the night stories would be over.

Before going to sleep, I knelt down and talked to the good god of heaven who carried me home safely. Although I was very tired and weary from traveling, I could not easily fall asleep that night. Various thoughts flashed across my mind concerning the future of my life. And even though my parents said nothing to me in regard to my returning home, I knew something strong was brewing in my father's mind, and it was certainly not coffee; but I perceived that my hour was not yet come, so I uttered not a word to anyone. There is a good old phrase stating "Silent River runs deep." My father's thoughts were very deep; he was perhaps drowning beneath the anger of my premature departure from the land of his birth. I thought, *how can I escape the path of my father's forthcoming whip of vengeance?*

For me, it was the longest night in history and a sleepless one too. I was very tense and filled with suspense, not knowing what shall befall me in the morrow. My mind was confused with numerous thoughts arising from the premature departure from my father's homeland and the possible consequences of my abrupt decision making to return home. That night was filled with sadness and sorrow; I travailed in the Spirit, seeking a favorable answer from God. It seemed like everyone was far from me, including God, and I was left alone to deliver myself from the agony of my burdens. I cried so loud, but it seemed no one could hear me. I felt like everything beneath me was caving in; my physical strength was failing, and my mind was confused. There was no sign of hope for tomorrow, no ray of light at the end of my invisible tunnel; the clock was striking on each hour, reminding me that the hour was near for me to enter my father's courtroom of justice. I needed God and needed him like never before because for me, it was Judgment Day approaching. So I spent most of the night meandering up and down the floor of my room like a wanted fugitive seeking for an escape route.

Early next morning, the cocks crowed loudly out in the meadow, and I awakened from my short slumber with a sudden rush of blood. Nevertheless, the beautiful sunrise shone brightly across the eastern skies, leaving a ray of light in my dark situational corner as I contemplated leaving my room. The glory of God's creation captivated my entire being when I peeped through the casement of my window. The old home scene of my early childhood came rushing down memory lane, and it was joy and sorrow in my heart, waiting for the next episode of my life with much apprehension.

My family was up early as usual; the mango season was in its highest peak, and as customary, the first one to rise would normally get the best of the crop. In the past, I was a prime candidate for the first-riser's position; but this time, I was completely out of the contest, nursing the psychological scars of my broken dreams while preparing for a showdown with my father. My brothers and sisters were back from the mango walk by the time I crawled out of the bed. The fun of picking up the mangos passed me by while I was lamenting the past hours of my sojourn and preparing for the next encounter with my parents—in particular, my father whom I feared the most.

It was shortly after breakfast that my horror began. The long, long night had passed, and the morning broke with a new day. There came the wrath of my parents, pouring out on me like a fountain of living stream. My father spilled out fury from his gut with uncontrollable anger, and this was the beginning of sorrow. He reached into his reserve storage and began to administer the stroke of the whip upon my back. He came at me fast and furious. I was cornered. I had no escape route, and the lashes came crashing on my back like rain on thirsty land. He hit me so hard, dust came out of my shirt; the preserved Swibble jack whip came constantly across my sore back, stroke after stroke. It felt like my back was on fire, but my father was in no hurry to end his reign of terror on me.

He was on a rampage, like a madman, fearless and careless. I screamed, I yelled, but the whip came like flaming hell. Dad had me covered. I could not run, I could not hide, and he had me cornered inside the living room, with only breathing space available. His friend Tom was passing by, hearing the commotion; he stopped at the house to inquire what was going on. I was hopeful that a neighbor was coming to rescue me from my father's wrath; but to my surprise, Tom shouted mockingly, "Leave piece of his skin for me!" meaning my father should put on more of the whip on me, but not kill me. He was adding fuel to the fire, encouraging my father to hit me more. The saga continued with my father's onslaughts; he hit me right, he hit me left, and I was running out of breath. I dared not try to escape before he was finished with me, or else he would save the rest for later on. It was a morning of hell on earth. My father was getting out of control, and I knew I had to make a move, or else my tragic story would later be told. I struggled to get out of his tight grip on me. I was running out of space; my mom started crying. You would think that would break his heart; instead, it hardened it more, and he intensified the lashes. It seemed he had no plans to stop hitting me soon, so I had to escape before my day was turned to night. I dashed beneath his legs; he tried to apprehend me but was unsuccessful in his attempt. I knew then that I was perhaps taking the greatest chance of my life, escaping from my father's whip; but this was the chance I had to take in order to preserve my life, despite of the expected certain consequences.

The reason for the encounter with my father was that my parents were not satisfied with the report they received from my father's homeland in terms of school and general behavior. I tried desperately to defend myself, but to no avail; they would hear none of what I had to say. I had no lawyer to defend me in my father's self-imposed courthouse of justice. I had no say in the matter once the elders had spoken; that was all they needed to hear, and my side of the story became null and void irrespective of the facts. One of my sisters shouted, "Cleve, you went there and only brought shame and disgrace to our family!"

"What type of Christian are you?" Jean added. I was torn apart by these sharp rebukes, and I knew it was the beginning of sorrow.

Not many days later, the struggle began to intensify, with bonds of affliction from some of my own brothers and sisters who persecuted me daily, with a quest to put out my Pentecostal fire. But I was adamant in my position, with my faith turned toward becoming a member of the New Testament Church of God and my mind affixed on heaven.".."

Notwithstanding, the testing grew worse; and my younger brothers, in particular, were determined to bring my Pentecostal experience to a premature end at any expense. The testing became more and more severe, and then it took a new turn for the worse—it became personal.

My younger brothers, four of them to be exact—Webster, David, Wayne and Rohan—reined havoc and chaos on my personal properties, taking turns in breaking into my room when I was at work or school and took away my personal belongings, such as shoes, pants, shirts, and other thing pertaining to church. They made every effort to detour me from the path of Pentecostalism, but I was determined not to let them extinguish my spiritual fire in the face of certain adversities.

I recall one particular instance when I was invited to national convention of the New Testament Church of God by one of my sisters, Elred, who was a member of that church. It was a great opportunity for me since I wanted to be more acquainted with that august body of believers at 52 West Street. However, my golden dreams turned into nightmares because the new suit and shoes I had prepared to wear along with a new tie suddenly disappeared from my room. I later discovered that my brother Collie was the prime suspect. To add to that agony, on my way from work while I was passing through the busy town, he called to me from across the street; and to my surprise, he had my new suit and shoes on, accompanied by a bottle of Red Stripe Bear, sipping merrily as he walked down the street. My heart was broken in a thousand pieces that evening as I walked away with my head hanging low. It was that same day I planned to wear the suit to the national convention, but my hopes were shattered, and I had to purchase other clothing and shoe in the nick of time.

The Christian journey became seemingly unbearable for me, but I found comfort in the scriptures and songs of the church. I felt like a prodigal son who came home to his father but was rejected. I left home long ago and had returned with a new conviction and a desire to serve the Lord. This, of course, brought an intense testing to my Christian faith; and my anticipated joy was turned to mourning at the expense of my father. I felt the pangs of hell hanging over me, and the foundation beneath my feet was shifting like quicksand. I knew I needed God to comfort me in those terrible times of my life, so I sought Him diligently on a daily basis with a view that He would deliver me out of my wilderness of sorrow and sighing. He answered my prayers and assured me of His comfort and protection, so I was held together by His mercies.

Here I was choosing to suffer afflictions at home than to dwell in the land of my father's birth for another season. The Holy Spirit brought grace to me in these trying moments of my life, and I found comfort in the words of God for my long, burdensome journey. I had no one to lean on but Jesus, who was my way maker, my comfort and shepherd. When folks turned against me, I looked unto the hills from whence cometh my help (Psalm 121:1). In God were my strength and His strength persevered me in an unfriendly world. When I was down in the valley of despair, God raised me up, and I could walk on mountains. He gave me a song in my dark midnight, and when I could not call Him, He came and rescued me from my enemies.

My trials were many and sometimes unbearable, but fasting and prayer held me close to the Pentecostal heritage. I was determined to preserve the Christian faith with all of my life for the good of the succeeding generations. The testing of my faith could not overcome the prompting of the Spirit within my spiritual bosom. I was driven by a divine compulsion that made me do the things I would not normally have done. Most persons knew me as a very quiet lad, but when the Spirit came upon me, there was a difference. I was an ordinary country boy doing extraordinary things for God.

Despite many efforts to rid myself of the persecution from my brothers, the trials and provocations became an addiction like thorns in my flesh until I decided to use reverse psychology on them in order to ease my burdens. Therefore, I pretended that I did not know when my personal belongings were missing from my room and replaced them accordingly even though it was an expensive venture. My father was a silent observer during this trying moment of my life and was now convinced that I was a true Christian because I took no actions against my brothers, and this was very puzzling to him, knowing the person I was before my conversion. He said, "There must be some god in you, boy. Why you are so calm? Seems like you have change for real"

As usual, we all attended my mom's church, which was the Love Lane Church of God. My mom was very pleased to have me in her company and proud of her son embracing the Gospel she had been preaching for many years to her children. She was actually counting on me to take over the mantle from her in that particular congregation in the years to come. However, I was looking in a different direction, unknown to her. This was the direction of the New Testament Church of God a few blocks down the road, which was called the Battle Factory Church due to the fact that a great worrier in the Gospel, the late Rev. Mrs. Carmen Taylor, many years before, had transformed the soda factory into the house of God.

Even though I had not yet received my water baptism, many plans were on the way for my future activities in my mom's church. To them, I was a promising young man with a bright future, and they planned to do everything in their power in order to keep me in that particular church. Those folks there were great people of God, loving and caring, not to mention the then pastor, the Reverend R. C. McNally; he was a man with an unending passion for the youths. He was optimistic about engrafting me into full-time ministry at a very early stage of my Christian development. In this same period of my life, I was caught in a conflict between my mom's church and the Battle Factory Church down the road, and I found myself leaning strongly in the direction of the latter.

While attending the church of God at love lane, I would always find time to sneak away to the Battle Factory Church before the service ended. This was not so pleasing to my mom at all; she wanted me to be settled in one church, and this meant the church that she was a part of. It was a long and painful religious battle for me, but I was determined in my mind to be a part of that old-fashioned church down the road. There were various moments of disagreements between my parents and me in regard to which church I should be a part of. I had my time of strong crying, praying, and planning regarding my ultimate intention. My whole life was placed in the judgment hall of my parents' religious courtroom for serious discussion when my father issued a warrant for me to appear in his self-proclaimed court of justice to answer charge concerning my own baptismal rites.

The struggles continued; my mind was like a literal battlefield, tossing to and fro, confused by the contestants of this religious arguments. In my subconscious mind, I was thinking of that day when I would step into the water for that outward identification with Christ, and in the same breath, there was the consciousness of the sin of disobedience and what would befall me if I was to be baptized without the knowledge of my parents. However, I took a firm grip of myself, mapped out my plans, and encouraged my soul. I was now more determined to break away from the popular opinions of the day and to register a personal statement to the observers. Meanwhile, my mom's church had eyes on me for the ministry and was hoping that I would take up the offer in the near future to study theology at Henderson

College, Indiana, in the United States of America. The church was willing to give me a full scholarship in the pursuit of my theological education. This offer was very appealing to me; it was a wonderful opportunity for me to embark upon the ministry of Gospel proclamation and to soar to new heights in Christian education, but there was a force greater than my intellect that was pulling me in another direction.

This particular direction was Pentecostalism, one of the trademarks of the Apostolic Age. And though despised and somewhat rejected by those who opposed the path I was contemplating, I remained steadfast in my quest toward the New Testament Church of God. Several baptisms passed; I was still in the waiting, not wanting to disobey my parents. I felt robbed of that sacred privilege of the religious ordinance of baptism. It was now three years since I accepted Christ as my personal savior, but I was not yet baptized. Scripturally speaking, baptism is required after one accepted Christ, and then one is received into the membership of the church. So I inquired privately from my sister Elred, who was a member of Battle Factory Church, "When would be the next baptism at your church?" She had no knowledge that I was about to break the laws of my God-fearing parents, but my mind was made up, and I had no intention to continue in this struggle. When I finally told her of my plans to get baptized, her joy was multiplied; she rejoiced with me after hearing the good news.

My focus was much clearer, and my decision was final. I was contended to make an end to the struggles for my soul's salvation and to secure a house of worship to call my own. There was no thought of retrieving from this final decision, despite of the various conscientious objectors. The date was set on the calendar of my mind; the time was relevant for my situation that baptism at the Battle Factory Church was to be held at five o'clock in the morning, just before the sun rises. The baptismal service was schedule for Good Friday morning, April 8, 1977. I felt like there were springs in my steps when the Reverend F. A. Beason, the then pastor, announced the baptismal service, for me, that service was to mark the turning point in my religious life. Notwithstanding, the terror I would face if my secret plans to be baptized in New Testament Church of God had come to the attention of my parents before the scheduled date. So I kept all my plans at a low profile. I told no one about this secret. I wanted to keep it free from the ears of the observers of my life so as not to be entangled in the bitter yoke of religious denominational bondage. As customary, I would have attended candidate's classes; but I deliberately restrained myself from doing so because I was too afraid that my parents would find out my plans, which could lead to my downfall in light of my parents' objection of me becoming a member of the noisy Battle Factory Church, the New Testament Church of God, a few blocks down the road from their church.

The time of the baptism drew nearer and nearer. There were anxious moments in my life, with a view to capture that glorious day of personal fulfillment. That particular week leading up to Good Friday was filled with anxiety, serious thinking, and even personal inner struggles as I sought God and His will for my life. Finally, I realized that I was on a path of no return that led to the blessed New Testament Church of God and, ultimately, the kingdom of an eternal abode. I was joyful but scared, not knowing how my parents would react to the situation when they learn that I am baptized in another church. The next few days leading up to Good Friday were filled with expectancy, both negative and positive. A thousand thoughts flashed through my fragile mind, which was already overwhelmed with silent thinking. I felt like a wandering lost sheep seeking for a home. However, the god of love was with me and strengthened me on my journey.

Then came Good Friday morning; that glorious day of spring, I woke up at four o'clock, got dressed, took my bag that was packed with clothes and hidden away from the night before, and crept quietly through the back door of my parents' house. Everyone was fast asleep; I made sure that no one knew I was out of bed at that frightening hour. The dew that fell overnight was evident on the ground that cold Good Friday morning. I felt the moisture on the green grass outside as I walked quietly past my parents' bedroom window. I kept my head down all the way until I cleared the length of the house. I held my bag with the baptism clothes tightly to my bosom and ran swiftly down the hill until at last I was out of sight.

Almost breathlessly, I dashed through the dark narrow track down the steep and lonely hill of the home scene until at last I reached the main road. As I traveled down Spring Bank Road, it was so silent you could hear a pin drop in the dark. I sought the help of the good Lord in my waking meditation and concentrated on the memories of the cross and the meaning of Good Friday and the savior who died on the cruel cross for my sins. The road was so dark you could almost feel the thickness of the predawn. It was about three and a half miles from my parents' house to the Battle

Factory Church on foot, and I had to be there before five o'clock for the pre-baptismal service. I hastened my steps, singing songs of melody in my heart as I journeyed to the church. A great joy came over me and drove my fears away. I could not comprehend the peace and calm I felt that early morning. It seemed that God came down and walked beside me while I was on my way to the church.

I waited for three long years to take the water baptism, and now my heart was inching closer to a time of spiritual jubilation. When I finally arrived at the church, it was a few minutes past five o'clock, and the saints were praying to God in a concert prayer. I heard an old veteran of the faith, Mother Linda Scott, calling out my name in prayer to God. Suddenly, warm tears began to flow from my eyes; they were tears of joy, knowing that I was about to take the step that would change my religious direction forever. My fears were gone, my mind was clear, my decision was final. On that morning of spring, the saints of God laid hands upon me and prayed an anointed prayer over my life. I was then asked to share my testimony in the midst of a vast congregation with numerous onlookers outside the church building observing what was going on inside the beautiful sanctuary that early hour of the morning

I felt like my feet were shaking. I was nervous, shy, and apprehensive standing in front of such a vast crowd to share my story. However, on the other hand, I was very excited and anxious to share what the Lord had done in my young life. The Lord gave me boldness to speak that morning; and the people were delighted to hear how the good Lord has brought me from out of my bondage, sorrow, and pain. I felt the anointed power of God upon me when I began to speak, and tears of joy kept rolling down my boney cheeks as I thought of the goodness of God. In my closing speech I implored others to follow me in serving the Lord Jesus Christ as their personal savior.

After the short service ended, we commenced a march from the Battle Factory Church to Bryan's Bay where the baptism was to take place. The people came from all walks of life and merged upon West Street, destined for the beautiful beach, about a mile away. They began to sing, play guitars and tambourines, and clap their hands with a passion that I had never seen before. As we journeyed on, others joined the massive throng along the way, and the momentum began to build up more and more. The pastor, Rev. F. A. Beason (FAB: Wash White and Clean), as he was affectionately called, led the procession, followed by the candidates all dressed in white; and then the musical band followed along with the great singers. You could hear a crescendo of praise going up to God from a great distance as the jubilant crowd passed through the respective towns and villages of East Portland.

When we arrived at Bryan's Bay, the morning was cold and bleak, but the beauty and splendor of God's creation was manifested across the ocean's bay. The glorious outstretched sky seemed to have covered the sinful villages of humanity and hid our calamities from the face of the holy creator of the universe. Soon, the baptismal service began, close to the brink of the ocean. The jubilant early-morning crowd started singing and clapping their hands and their tambourines. A cold breeze blew over the bay, but the blessed saints kept the fire burning inside their souls, ringing out the songs of Zion. As for me, my mind was made up, my record was clear, and my spirit was steadfast, despite of the threat of the enemy. So I joined the band of happy Christians down by the seaside of Bryan's Bay to show the world that I was gone from sin and shame to live for Christ and to share his precious name to every man I meet along the way

The baptismal service was now in full gear; several candidates were immersed into that chilly water of Bryan's Bay. I was very anxious, yet apprehensive. A numerous thoughts flashed through my mind as my time to be baptized drew nearer. I waited patiently while the candidates before me entered the chilly water to be baptized by the pastor F. A. Beason. Some amount of fear suddenly came over me. I talked to myself silently, *What if one of my family members is among this vast crowd and sees me preparing to be baptized this morning?* I pondered quietly in my heart about changing my mind about this baptismal service. The devil was on my case, trying to confuse me. He was saying, "What if someone at home found out that you have left home this morning?" I was next in line, behind my cousin Brother Michael Coulson. So I walked close to him toward the water. I stepped into the deep blue ocean of Bryan's Bay. Pastor Beason welcomed me into the kingdom of Christ, and I felt elated, the glorious moment I yearned for has finally come. The Reverend Fedlyn A. Beason held me by the hand and asked me to repeat the baptismal vow. I exclaimed, "Thy vows O Lord remain upon me until death" this was a serious vow that I had to take publicly, to show the world that I was identifying myself with Christ and the believers and was denouncing the sins of my past.

I had to repeat this vow three times aloud; then the pastor instructed me to clasped my hands, and he turned is eyes toward the heavens and said with a loud voice, "Brother Aubrey Brown, upon the confession of your faith and by the authority vested in me as a servant of the Lord Jesus Christ and as a minister the church of God, I now baptize you in the name of the Father and of the Son and of the Holy Spirit." Then he plunged me beneath the waters; and I came up rejoicing in the god of my salvation shouting, "Hallelujah! Praise the Lord!" My mouth was filled with praises to the Almighty God for having brought me through the storm clouds of yesterday. I could not have held back the spontaneous joy that flowed from my inner being, which filled my soul with unending adorations to the god of the universe. It was a golden dream come true for me on that blessed morning when I was baptized, I came up out of the chilly waters of Bryan's Bay; that unforgettable moment of irrevocable joy kept streaming down the corners of my joyful Christian life and left me with unquenchable momentum as I walked the coveted pathway of Christendom with glorious certainty.

I clearly recalled that day when the saints rejoiced with me, especially those who knew the struggles I had gone through in my early Christian journey. My heart was stirred, my soul was revived, my strength was renewed on that early morning of spring when into the water I forgot my past and reached unto the future with God, who pardoned my sins and forgave my iniquities. In that great moment, the devil was still on my track, trying to drive fear in my heart, haunting me with the thought of going home to face the wrath of my relatives—in particular, the fury of my farther, whom I feared the most on earth. However, the good Lord gave me courage as I traveled along, praying in my heart that God would change my daddy someday.

After the baptismal service, we marched back to the church from Bryan's Bay, singing and rejoicing through the streets of the city. The sun was out in all its glory and the sleeping folks in town were now up and about doing their chores. The jubilant crowd of Christian soldiers drew the attention of the villagers, and soon, some of them joined the procession. Another service known as Good Friday Service began shortly after we reached the church; this was usually a power-packed celebration of worship, with personal testimonies and a keynote address from the pastor usually on the subject of the Crucifixion of our Lord Jesus Christ. It was a time of reflection and repentance when the believers would pour out their hearts to the Lord in thansgiving.

There was a great intervention of the Holy Spirit in the church that morning, but I was consumed by a heavy burden, which threatened to cut short my rejoicing in God. I knew I had to face the music of my father's whip when I return home that morning of spring; and from personal experiences, it was no use fooling myself, so I prepared my mind to deal with whatsoever was coming my way. The service ended shortly after midday. I was hoping that it would never end, at least not in a million years; only then I would be safe from the long arm of my father's law. I knew I had to walk three and a half miles home, but I was in no hurry to get there. I was trying to delay what I had to face upon returning home. Notwithstanding, in my mind, I was prepared to face whatever might come my way, not on my own, but by the grace of God.

Upon reaching home, I first came into contact with one of my elder sisters, Jean, who was washing clothes under the huge stringy mango tree. I politely said, "Good afternoon, sister Jean."

She gave me a suspicious smile; and suddenly, there came the large wash pan of soap and water on top of my head, streaming down on my suit, in my eyes, ears, and mouth. She said, "You were not baptized good enough this morning, so let me baptize you again." It was at this point that I knew the news of my baptism had reached my home, and I sensed that trouble was ahead. While I was trying to clear my blurred vision, as a result of the soap water, I felt some serious blows all over my body like someone wanted to take the life out of me. I tried to take evasive action, but more and more, there came a barrage of large green mangoes—pelting me from all angles. I ran as fast as I could, trying to get to the veranda of the house, ducking and slipping from the weapons of mass destruction that flew closely to my head and my eyes. It was the mercies of God that kept me from serious harm at the hands of my younger brothers, who were expressing their disapproval about my baptism. If I had not taken steps to protect myself, I would've probably ended up in the *general hospital* at the hands of the *young and restless* that seemed to be living in *another world* in those *days of my life*. Those unsaved brothers of mine were lurking in the mango tree, awaiting my arrival with a view to attack my confidence in God and my determination to walk in the Christian way of life; but I survived the baptism of my sister Jean and the blows from those tough green mangoes from my younger brothers, who pushed me to the brink of discouragements.

Soon, it was quite evident that there was no safe haven at home. Shortly after this ordeal, I ran into the path of my father. This was the capstone of my post baptism trials and tribulation. It would seem that God quenched my father's fire and subdued his temper, so I escaped unhurt, free from the crack of his whip. I knew I had done a good thing when I was baptized; on the other hand, the devil wanted me to feel like I have done a bad thing because I broke my parents' order, sneaking away on that early morning to be baptized. My dad kept his cool for a while, my mom uttered a few words of disappointment, and my younger brothers seized the opportunity to persecute me on every angle of my life. There were times when I felt like Joseph in the Old Testament, who was placed in the pit to die by his brothers. They mocked and tested my faith in God to see if I would surrender to the devil and lose my composure. But I held firm to my godly conviction and would not let down my guard for nothing.

It was a great struggle against all odds; I had to fight the good fight of faith on the Good Friday morning. As a result of me taking my water baptism, I suffered greatly and sometimes felt like I had committed a crime and was now facing the consequences. Soon, most of the family made a unanimous decision to condemn my action. Some criticized, others ostracized, and everyone played their part on the stage of opposition, acting out their anger and dissatisfaction. I had my fair share of trials rendered to me from all angles, and I faced them alone; there was no one on my side of the fence, but I was persuaded that God would see me through. The testing continued for the rest of the day and into the others that followed. On the next Sunday, while I was getting ready for church, I soon discovered that some of my belongings such as shoes, pants, or shirts were missing from my closet. My younger brothers were not afraid to claim responsibility for the missing items from my room; in fact, to them, it was their greatest pleasure to test my faith by snatching away my personal properties.

After seeing how I reacted to the trials, my father was becoming more and more convinced that I was a changed person and indeed a true believer in the Lord. He knew that if it were not so, there would have been some serious repercussions in the family home on that weekend of the holy season. Normally, I would have retaliated violently under those circumstances, but I was grounded in my belief in God and was becoming more mature in the Christian walk of life. So I endured that hardship as a brave soldier of the cross. It was evident that there was a great change in my attitude; my heart was transformed by the Holy Spirit, and my foundation was routed in the Word of God.

Previously, I was very anxious to leave my father's homeland to return to my native land, but now there was mixed feelings within me. "I have jumped out of the frying pan into the fire." On the other hand, I knew there was no place like home sweet home. Everything seemed different from before. I left the old home scene, and I had to get myself reacquainted with my home again. The time and seasons have changed rapidly, and it was up to me to adapt, so I pondered in my heart which way to take in the days and weeks ahead. There were times when I felt like returning to the Garden Parish, with a view to escape the testing of my faith at the hands of my younger brothers. But like Moses, it was better to suffer the afflictions at home than to return to the homeland of my dad for another season. So I remained contented in whatsoever state I was in, endeavoring to fight manfully onward in Christ Jesus, knowing that He will keep me in perfect peace. The memorable Good Friday morning was transformed into a Black Friday when I arrived home from the baptismal service; dark clouds of spiritual struggles came rushing down my mental skies, with a view to block my vision of the heavenly king. But with a determined spirit, I pressed onward to the prize before me with great joy.

I was encouraged by the thought that whatever would befall me after I had taken my water baptism would not be able to be compared with the joy of the blessed fellowship of the saints in Christ. So I went on, knowing that God would see me through. For it was the same God who kept me in my father's homeland, and I knew He was with me and will be with me to the end of the ages. The trials continued constantly from my younger brothers, in all forms of provocations, traps and snares; but my mind was made up. I would not turn back because I wanted to see my Jesus someday. My anchor held, my future was bright, my head was held upward, and my face was set toward the portals of glory, my final home. And when I reached that final home at last, where the golden bells would ring to welcome me, I'd sing and shout with joy aloud and tell the nations of the world how God had saved my soul from sin and opened heaven's gate that I might come in.

The Gift of God

After settling down in my hometown, I began to search the scriptures steadfastly on a daily basis. I was trying to find the deep mysteries of God in the books of the prophets. Fasting and prayer were the most common practice of the church of God that I attended, and the study of the Word was mandatory in that particular church. While concentrating on the prophetic gifts recorded in the Bible, I began to do some serious studying. My heart was leaning toward the gift of the Spirit with an ambition to be equipped with that heavenly legacy. Then I read that "God worked upon the desires of a man's heart." I wanted to prove this for myself, so I began a journey into the unknown by soliciting God on a regular basis in order to be endowed with one of the spiritual gifts. This motivated me to seek the Lord with all that was in me. I needed to hear from God for myself what gift He would bestow upon me for the Christian service.

I knew that God often heard the cry of His people and granted them their desires. Therefore, it was my time to prove him in a personal way. In my prayers, I requested of the Lord to make me a John the Baptist to cry in the wilderness of my country against sin and injustice, or an Elijah to pray the fire down from heaven that people may know the true and living God. With a convincing heart, I sought the Lord on this matter; like Jacob, I would not let go of God until I get an answer. At this point in my life, I knew I needed more of God in order to survive the raging tides of temptation that haunted me like a persistent ghost. So there was more reason than one to seek the gift and power of God. On Tuesdays, my friends and I would witness to our unsaved friends on the streets of the city. We would hand out Gospel tracts and preach on public buses from one community to another.

Every Wednesday was set aside for prayer and fasting. I had my own team of disciples made up of dedicated and consecrated young people: there were Trevor, Blue, Duffus, Pat, Cynthia, Dennie, Michael, and myself. Our goal was to plunder hell in order to populate heaven. We traveled the countryside districts, proclaiming the good news of salvation, laying hands on the sick, and casting our demons from the lives of people. We were heaven-bound, Holy Spirit filled, and fearless in our pursuit to deliver those that were bound and oppressed by Satan. The enemies of God did not make it easy for us in our sojourn; he organized with his agents to destroy the work we set out to accomplish in God's vineyard. However, the courageous team of Christian ambassadors kept going, telling the good news everywhere we went until soon many were converted and received the baptism of the Holy Spirit. The awesomeness of God's love was demonstrated in our lives. The people were told about God's coming judgment and were given instructions how they may escape His impending doom. My desire was to be used by God to help my countrymen find the way to God. So I sought God earnestly for His gift in my life.

One particular Wednesday as we journeyed with the Gospel of salvation, the Holy Spirit led us to a place called Clear Spring, near the District of Drapers, to a house where a woman was very sick, unto death, lying on her bed for three weeks; she was unable to move by herself. The team was introduced to the member of the household who welcomed us inside. Some of the household members were busy cooking, washing, and doing other things. The Spirit of the Lord moved upon Trevor, who requested that all members of the family join us in prayer for the sick woman lying in affliction. We began to sing "Where He Leads Me, I Will Follow." Then the Holy Spirit began to manifest in us. I was moved to tears when I looked at the woman's bewildered countenance; she was in anguish and pain. The prayer of faith was prayed, and the Holy Spirit intervened. Cynthia then read Ezekiel 37:8: "And when I beheld, lo, the sinews and the flesh came up upon them, and the skin covered them above: but there was no breath in them."

After this, we sang "Sweet will of God", and the Holy Spirit came more forceful upon us in the room; then suddenly, the woman jumped up on her feet and began to run all over the house, praising God. She was healed by the power of God. I felt like the house vibrated. My feet felt like they were completely off the ground when the anointing fell on me in that room. I was taken into the splendor of God's glory. The Spirit of God was speaking to me, but I did not understand because I was young in Christ Jesus. I felt like fire was inside of me burning out my inner man, and I heard a voice like the roar of waters from a steep hill. The Holy Spirit bid me to touch the woman on her head, and as soon as I did so, she began to speak in heavenly tongues; she was baptized with the Holy Spirit of God. I soon felt the prompting of the Spirit in my spiritual bosom, telling me what to say to His people in that household. I tried to resist the Spirit, and Sister Pat Bell cried out, "Quench not the Spirit of God and speak the Word of the Lord, Brother Brown!"

Then suddenly, the words came forcefully out of my mouth. "Thus said the Lord, God of heaven, repent and turn away from your wicked ways. And the Lord thy God shall give you life, and you shall serve Him all your days." Like a cloudburst, you could hear spontaneous shouting in the hills of Drapers from this woman's house. Deliverance came not only to the woman, but also to me. The Lord used me greatly to prophesy. This was explained to me later by a member of the Gospel team, that I have received the gift of prophecy. I began to search the scripture from that day to find out what the gift of prophecy meant. From thereafter, I began to prophesy in the name of the Lord. For the rest of the week, I pondered in my heart on what had taken place at Clear Spring. Then the Lord spoke to me clearly and said, "I have given you what you asked of me." This was the confirmation that I needed to hear to clear all avenues of doubts and fear.

The following Sunday was youth Sunday at our church. The Spirit of the Lord moved upon me, and I prophesied the people were touched; some were amazed, and others looking on said, "Is this Mr. Brown's son?"

The pastor, Rev. F. A. Beason, shouted, "This is one of the gifts of the Spirit that was locking in the church for many years. Without the gifts of the Spirit, the church is not fully completed!" The congregation was elated; the Holy Spirit stirred the believers' hearts as revival flames blew across the audience that day in church. God was near to me, and I was near to Him; the relationship was close between God and me. His deep presence was always with me in the onward march of life. There are diversities of gifts mentioned in the Holy Bible, but God chose to give me the gift of prophecy, and I prophesied with a burden like Obadiah. I could actually feel the weight of the people's sin when I prophesied in church, and there was a burning in my soul as I spoke "Thus said the Lord."

There were even times when I wanted God to take away the gift from me because of the burden that came to me in the execution of this gift. Oftentimes, I prayed that He would remove the burden from my spiritual bosom and release me of the anguish of my soul as I lamented the sins of the people. The word of the lord keep coming to me daily and I prophesied as I was commanded, concerning sin, injustice in the nation sins of the national leaders, judgment and coming disasters upon the nation, such as hurricanes and earthquakes. The lord led me to prophesy for about one month consecutively about a coming earthquake, I saw in my spirit what was about to take place and warned the people, then suddenly one the prophesy came to pass when the earth shook, folks scampered for cover in the various cities and towns. History recorded that there were hundreds of people at the movie in the Delmar Theater in the city of port Antonio when the earth shook; some ran out into the street, others jumped into the sea trying to escape. After this, some of the people repented of their sins and surrendered to the lordship of Christ.

There were those critics who felt that I should keep quiet in church and not prophesy when special visitors came to worship with us. But there were times that I wished that God would ignore me and not let me prophesy at all, but there was no letting up with God on my path. If it was left up to me, I would keep quiet in church always, but I was not my own—I belonged to God. Some say I was mashing up the church and disturbing the community, but I was driven by a divine locomotion to do the things I did. It was a compulsive force that held me captive and would not let me go for nothing in this world. Then I discovered that it was an awful thing to fall into the hand of the living God. As I prophesied what God commanded me to say, great oppositions rose up against me within and outside the church. I was criticized, ostracized, mocked, scorned, and abused and was nicknamed 'Son of the Prophets'.

Those who tried to shut me up were spoken to by God, causing fear to come upon them; those who tried to stop me physically were electrocuted by the power of the Holy Spirit. I was told by an old veteran of the church, Mother Linda Scott, that she saw smoke come out of my mouth one night when I prophesied the Word of the Lord. The call of God was evident upon me, and my main duty was to act as a spokesman for God at a time when sin was rapidly increasing in the society and spreading like wildfire toward the church. My cool and calm personality was disrupted by the dynamite of God, revealing the sinful acts of men in the congregation of the saints.

The opposing enemies of my soul were soon made silent by God in the days that followed. We beheld the matchless wonders of God's eternal grace unfold in the lives of sinful men as the Spirit led them to the altar of repentance. My argument was that God put his Holy Spirit into earthly vessels to accomplish heavenly things when He led captivity captive and gave gifts unto men. I discovered that God's gifts to men are not collections of heavenly souvenirs, but rather an everlasting investment for the edification of the saints that are in Christ Jesus. I received the gift of prophecy, a gift I had prayed for a long time ago. The Lord honored my request, and I learned that I must be careful what I asked for because it may just come to me. I never knew what was coming with the gift, and when I tried to return it to God who gave it, He did not grant me my request. Instead, He gave me message after message to deliver to His people.

I sometimes felt like Jonah wanted God to destroy the people for their sins, but He let me know that He was "rich in mercy and slow to judgment." So I went away with my head hung low at the rebuke of the Lord, recognizing that I am only a servant driven by divine compulsion to speak the message of Jehovah wherever and whenever He would have me to speak. Therefore, I soon recognized that the gift of God is irrevocable, and God was depending on me to carry out my God-given task despite of the burden that was upon me.

CHAPTER SIX

BURDENS ON MY JOURNEY: PART TWO

As a young man, courage was the watchword in those dark days of temptation. The memories of the past events haunted me. I was oftentimes abused and misused by my own brethrens. The dark days overshadowed the sunlight of hope on the horizon of my twisted thoughts. There were criticizers and opposing folks who constantly afflicted my battered mind with their new methods of testing designed to tear my soul asunder. But persistency was in my favor, and I proceeded by faith in the onward march of life. The hand of the Lord was upon me like His hand was upon Elijah, and Satan did not like it at all, so he got angry and set my own country folks against me. God knew the desires of my heart, and His comforting arms undergirded me, reminding me of the written words "Lo, I am with you always, even unto the end of the world" (Matthew 28:20).

The more I prophesied in the name of the Lord, the more opposition grew against me. But I counted all things unimportant that the power of God may rest upon me. At one stage, I was completely stressed out. I began to lose weight rapidly because the appetite for food had gone from me. Some of my relatives forsook me others cited me as a treat to the family's reputation I wandered through the wilderness of consideration like a pilgrim detoured from the path to Mecca. In these trying moments, I found the courage to pray and the cause to endure hardships. I set my eyes on the cross of Calvary on which the savior died. The searchlight of the Holy Spirit was upon my life. I cried for mercy, and God heard my despairing cry. There was literal confrontation from within and outside the church on a regular basis by individuals who opposed my spiritual enlightenment from God through the prophetic utterance of my stammering tongue. Some members of my own family were not inclined to my style of Pentecostal worship and prophetic proclamation. My rise to the peak of Pentecostalism created various indifferences in my family, which sometimes led to animosity, religious family feuds, and numerous indignities.

Like the prophet Elijah in the Old Testament, I felt I was left alone and that all the other prophets were dead, so I thought. I too wanted to die and quickly too, but God let me know that "the journey has just begun." My soul burned within me as I faced the conflicts and opposition from within the church and at home. One particular Sunday, the Spirit of the Lord came heavily upon me and led me out of my seat in the aisles of the church and bid me to prophesy to the congregation concerning their shortcomings. After the service ended, I was confronted, ridiculed, mocked, and denounced by some members and unbelievers alike. Like Elisha, some children mocked me, saying "Thus said the Lord" each time they passed by me; and that became my nickname. But I did not curse them like the prophet. Instead, I forgave them and prayed for them, for they knew not what they were doing.

There were times when I was literally afraid of my own folks and even of my own self. When the Spirit came upon me, I would prophesy as the Lord directed me. I was driven by a force that was compulsive. I had no choice but to accept the command of God in the call for the prophetic proclamations. There were the naturalists who thought I was going crazy because they could not understand the things of the Holy Spirit. Some of the old veterans of the faith in the congregation at the Battle Factory Church encouraged me to sound the alarm in the holy mountain of God without fear or favor. Chief among them were Sister Linda Scott, who told me, "You are under the rock, and the rock is higher than you."

Mother McKenzie said, "When you lay this old cross down, you shall receive a shining crown."

Brother Alexander Brady patted me on the shoulder and said, "Just keep a cool head, my brother."

And Sister Collette Mitchell told me, "God walks the dark hills to guide my footstep." and Sister Joan Scott reminded me that "the king is coming"

These saints of God gave me strength for my journey. The words that came from the mouths of those choice servants of the Lord pushed me further in the cause of Gospel preaching.

The testing of my faith continued steadfast, and each time when it seemed that burdens were lifted, I was reminded that it was only the beginning of my sorrow. God in His mercy kept me strengthened for the labor; there were many sleepless nights and sorrowful days of prolonged persecutions. My spiritual skies once more became foggy, and my visions were dark and dismal. I stumbled like an old man coming down the prime of his life, with shaking knees and stammering speech. The unforgettable memories of my daily religious persecutions cleaved to the core of my life and perhaps delayed the comfort of my tomorrow as I fought for the cause of righteousness. I sought God earnestly in prayer and fasting, requesting that He would take the gift of prophecy from me and set me free from the plague that haunted my soul. However, the more I sought God, the more He showed me the sins of the people; and I had to cry against sin and injustice.

I could not escape the call of God to the prophetic office no matter how hard I tried to rid myself of His command to prophesy. I was caught between two dreaded columns of my Christian life—*to pray or not to pray*. If I didn't, I would have neglected the Christian's duty; and if I did, God would endow me to do some things that were against the natural laws of earth, which is not consistent to human's thoughts but will subsequently edify the Body of Christ. The enemies of my soul were bent on stirring up the spirit of division so as to hinder the work of Christ.

One bright and beautiful summer morning, my father was riding his bicycle to town when a lady intercepted him. He got off his bicycle to hear what she had to say; with a polite "Good morning," she began her story. "Mr. Brown," she said mannerly, "your son seems like he is trying to mash up the church. Maybe he wants to take over. Please warn him for me, Mr. Brown." Then she walked away from the scene with disgust.

My father was not amused when he related the story to the rest of the family. No defense was good enough for me to present to my father on that day. He was furious; some family members were certainly disturbed by the latest news concerning me. I was mocked and provoked by some of my brothers and sisters. One of my elder sisters, Jean, said, "If you had stayed in your parents' church, you would be better off today. You begged for what is happening to you now." The devil was mad because the Lord used me to prophesy to the church concerning the deeds of the people. This complaint from that disgruntled member of the church was lodged by the woman who was guilty of the sins I prophesied against, and the enemy was trying to destroy my reputation by slanderous accusation.

However, I held the steering wheel of my soul in the right direction toward the highway of prayer and fasting.

At this point in my life, the Lord began to reveal himself to me more clearly. I had visions of things that were shortly to come to pass in my day and time. I had the Spirit of discernment and could see things beyond the natural when endued by the Holy Spirit, and the mysteries of godliness were shown to me by divine intervention upon my finite eyes, making me see extraordinary things.

One night, I had a vision; in my vision, I saw thirty-six beautiful young girls standing in a green pasture. Suddenly, there appeared one young girl standing by herself a few yards away from the others. Then a voice out of the clouds spoke these words to me, "All those shall turn away from you, but the one standing far off shall be a multitude of happiness and peace to you. Hearken to my voice, for I am the Lord." Then suddenly, this strange girl walked toward me, and I awoke out of the vision with fear and trembling. The other girls I clearly recognized as members of the Battle Factory Church I attended, but the other was a stranger. I could not understand the mystery of this vision, so I sought help from the elders of the church, who interpreted the vision to mean that God was preparing a bride for me. I was totally amused when I received the interpretation of the vision, but I had to keep the amusement to myself as these saints were the spiritual authority of the church; therefore, disregarding this interpretation would be deemed as a religious sacrilege.

I was spiritually oriented; my mind was set on heaven. I had the utmost respect for these saints but was skeptical of the interpretation. My inclination was that the Lord would come before I even thought of getting married. The spirituality of the church was of a high standard at the time under the dynamic leadership of the then pastor, the Reverend F.A. Beason. Therefore, the ideas and thoughts of earthly enjoyment seemed unwelcomed among the young people of that era. Fasting and prayer, Bible studies, and the worship of Jehovah took center stage in our lives. It was the high point of the history of Battle Factory Church, popularly known as Mr. Beason's Church in that city even until today.

One Sunday night, as the great man of God Rev. F.A. Beason took his stand to preach, I saw a flaming circle of fire around his head descending to his feet. His entire countenance suddenly became like that of an angel, and the power of God shook the congregation with a majestic supernatural force that was not common to man. I felt an unusual power of God; some of the saints were slain by the Holy Spirit. It was a night of heaven on earth; the Holy Spirit came upon me and carried me in the midst of the congregation. I felt like my feet were off the ground. The Spirit came rapidly, like the dashing waters of Dunn's River Falls.

I was at the peak of spiritual ecstasy; notwithstanding, there were more persecutions than ever before. But as the saying goes, "The higher the monkey climbs, the more him expose." Satan was after me, like lion seeking for a prey for a midnight snack. A mighty throng of opposition came against me, and my soul began to grieve in tumults of distress; my mind was overcrowded with numerous thoughts. I was footsore and weary from traveling the Gospel road, but God kept me intact and in route to the New Jerusalem.

There was a stern battle for supremacy between the Spirit and the flesh in the jungle of my conflictions. I pondered on the grace of God that brought my salvation. There were times when I felt like giving up the race; but my best friend, Trucky, was always there to encourage me on the journey. He was a source of inspiration to me when the going got tough in my life. We usually spent long hours on the road traveling from Battle Factory Church to Spring Bank, talking about the blessings after each church service. Sometimes we would talk until the day broke. Mother Curtis, Trucky's mom, was always there with a word of advice and encouragement each time we traveled home together.

As the religious sojourn continued, my secular life was also afflicted by the boisterous winds of temptation from my younger brothers, who plundered my wardrobe without mercy, removing my newest items of clothing and footwear by false entry into my room. And to add to this injury, they had the audacity to confront me when I made known my dissatisfaction. This was becoming unbearable for any human to endure, but God promised that His "grace was sufficient for me." Had it not been for the grace of God and the strong prayers of the folks that wished me well, my conversion to Christianity would have been excluded from the historical and religious archives of the ecclesiastical organization. And my dream of entering God's employment would have ended in a nightmare beside the eternal gate of individual damnation. God's Spirit was very much persistent upon me. Therefore, my salvation was not forsaken, and my calling was not terminated.

Although the mingled burdens kept moving from one end of my life to the other, some good folks at Battle Factory Church kept themselves on speaking terms with God on my behalf. I decided to fight manfully onwards, until that day when my tales will be told at the ending of my saga this heart of mine continued to burn like a raging fire. But I'll be glad when the day is done and night is passed; then my heavy burdens will be gone forever from this restless soul of mine. The agony of my burdens was upon me throughout my journey it seemed like my most difficult bridge to cross in order to get to the other side of true happiness and contentment. The god of all true providence was my pilot in good and bad times. When I was down, He carried me on His shoulder to a place of safety and covered me with His everlasting love.

My journey seemed relentless, full of struggles, tempests, and storms along the restless way; but the god of my soul kept me in perfect peace despite of the burdens on my journey. I was hinging toward the things of god with a passion for humanity and to help those I met along the way to the heavenly city. I had a great love for people and wanted to see them succeed in every aspect of their lives especially in finding eternal life for their souls. The unconditional love of god taught me to love my fellowmen as myself and I relish the privilege of serving others.

Falling In Love

My mind went wandering, far away, out in the wilderness of doubt and uncertainty. I sometimes felt dismayed as I struggled breathlessly through the jungle of life in my quest for survival. The valleys were deep and the mountains very steep; I was tangled in the web of some deep distress and anxious moments of dissatisfactions, mingled with uncertain days of undeniable sociological stress, trying to rid myself of the memories of the unforgettable arguments of yesteryears. Life had me struggling between sorrow and joy, between love and hate in my pursuits for happiness. Beyond the curtains of my personality were the bitter scars of past wounds that haunted my spirit like Indian ghosts. But I was determined once and for all to cleanse my thoughts of bad brats who sought to detour me from my heavenly destination.

Love was flying high like Christmas kites from the castle of my heart to the depths of my soul. I was caught in the winds of love that held me tight and would not let me go. The love of God was strong within me, burning like California's fire in the hot summer; that love was measureless and strong, even when things were sometimes going wrong. I had my mind fixed on the cross in those days; nothing seemed to stop me from going on with Jesus. I had my fair share of troubles since I accepted Jesus Christ as my personal savior. I had never been in love before; I was just a young and timid lad seeking for a passage to glory, condescending to men of low estate. I had no knowledge of intimate love; all I knew was the unmerited love of God. I never contemplated embarking upon the avenue of intimate love, but it came fast up my lonely stream and swept my feet off the ground with the sudden panting of my nervous heart.

I recalled the early days of childhood when I would secretly listen to my parents' conversation but most of the time could not understand the meaning of some of the phrases they used. For instance "falling in love," literally speaking, I thought it meant that someone had fallen into a trap and could not come out. However, as I grew older, it became clearer to me. I had school girlfriends; some were just traveling companions that usually walked with me home from school, and others were classmates whom I admired. A few of the girls had high hopes of capturing my heart, but I was very shy and naïve; and even if I did love one of them, I would not have a clue how to approach her. I was living in a world of my own, concentrating on the things of God and the church. It was clear that I was in a dream world then, and perhaps the age of adolescence had filled my heart with many eternal matters beyond my wildest dreams. Therefore I was out of touch with the love of the opposite sex

As the days went by, my heart began to grow fond of one of my schoolmates who lived in my district. Her name was Sonia Simmons. I began to feel something bubbling inside of me toward her, and soon, I was having a serious crush on her. However, I just could not find the courage to tell her how I felt about her. There were various opportunities for me to share this hidden secret with Sonia, but I did not have the slightest idea how to tell her or what to say to her concerning my love for her. I pondered about her in my heart when she was not in my presence but procrastinated about expressing my feelings each time I saw her angelic face. My love for her grew stronger. I suspected that she might have had an idea that I was trying to knock at her heart's door; but she too was very shy. It was two innocent teenagers coexisting in an era of strict religious parental shelter who had no knowledge of the subject of "falling in love." Sonia was deeply in love with me; I could see it in her eyes and felt the magnet of her heart attracting mine. Still, neither of us made any serious attempts to vocalize our intimate feelings toward each other until finally I lost her forever. After graduation, she told me that she was leaving town for good. My heart sunk in deep despair; it felt like she was gone forever. Unfortunately, I waited too long to express my feelings to Sonia, and now she was about to depart from my town and perhaps from my life for good. Subsequently, she moved out of town to the capital city of Kingston shortly after graduating from senior school. This was heartbreaking for me. I felt like my dreams were shattered and my hopes were gone. The truth was I had no one to blame but myself for not letting her know how I felt about her while she was at school and the various times we walked home together. I was young and filled with timidity. Sonia was gone, and I was left forlorn, missing the one I adored. Love had gone with the wind rent from the castle of a lonely heart, perhaps never to return to the place she once lived to hear the sound of love again. The truth is, for a while, I just couldn't get her out of my mind. My whole life seemed to fall apart when she departed for the capital city. At that particular time, I had the first glimpse of love, and now it was gone so soon. However, I decided to pick up the broken pieces and move along life's journey.

In those days, it was incumbent upon the believers to refrain from all impurities. We were told "to shun the very appearance of evil." Therefore, having a girlfriend was deemed as evil by the elders of the church. This was an unpardonable sin in the eyes of my parents; the church too had its rule on this matter. Based on my parents' teachings and rules, *falling in love* was the prerogative of married people only. According to my parents' unwritten laws, to have a girlfriend was a capital crime punishable in my father's courtroom of justice. The truth was that I had so much fear for God and my parents that I could not seriously mention that I had *fallen in love*; otherwise, I would be immediately reprimanded.

In the early seventies, when I became a member of the Battle Factory Church at 52 West Street, the congregation was on a notable spiritual high pinnacle; various persons received the baptism of Holy Spirit. There were numerous miracles of healing that took place, new converts added to the church weekly, and there was a mysterious movement of the Holy Spirit in the church. it was during the miraculous days of the remarkable years of Rev . . . F.B.Beason's administration, that the supernatural interventions of God were seen and felt in the city of Port Antonio like never before. It was reported that a dead boy came back to life in that church after Rev.Beason laid hand upon him and prayed to the god of heaven.

During that historic period of the church life, holiness was the trademark of the converted Christians. There were extraordinary manifestations of the Holy Spirit upon the saints. Strange things happened at the Battle Factory Church, which left onlookers spellbound, praying and weeping at the altar. Everyone mind was focused on the baptism of the Holy Spirit and the return of Jesus Christ. I was not concerned with any serious earthly occupation and certainly not about *falling in love* because I was too heavenly minded to concentrate on earthly things. I had heaven on my mind and was determined to reach there at any cost. The god of all times captivated my mind and set me on a path toward eternity. But I soon learned from my pastor, Rev. F. A. Beason (FAB Wash White and Clean) that if *I was too heavenly minded, I would be no earthly good.*

The church was filled with beautiful attractive young girls from all temperaments and backgrounds. I soon felt a quiver of love warming my heart for a damsel named Janet, who was an ardent youth worker in the Battle Factory Church. I tried very hard to dismiss the feelings of love from my converted mind, but it was more forceful than I thought; and soon, my heart began to yearn toward her. However, not long afterward, I learned that she too felt the same way about me. The subject of love came rushing down the corner of my mind as I began to develop a steady sociable relationship with Janet.

A few months passed, and with much apprehension on my path, I decided to have a little chat with Janet on the intriguing subject of love. We were good friends for some time, not even thinking of a relationship, so this was somewhat unusual for me to approach. On the other hand, she was a very pleasant young lady, one who was dedicated to God and the church in every sense of the word. Gradually, our friendship grew into a closer relationship until finally; an intimate sensation began to knock on the door of my heart with a sense of importunity. However, there was some amount of uncertainty on my path; perhaps I was too taken up with the things of God and His works until I was losing interest on earthly expectations.

I tried to muster some courage in order to have a serious talk with Janet concerning a possible relationship. I wanted to be sure that I was her favorite prospect for a possible future, and if not, I would know what course of action to take in the days ahead. Although I was driven by a divine compulsion, the feelings of love kept boiling up inside of me like a coming storm from the Mexican gulf. However, I could not find the guts to approach her. Janet was from the city; and I was a country boy from the hills of Spring Bank, living in the prime of my life, devoted to God and the church in my city, and was an integral part of Kingdom Building at 52 West Street, Port Antonio. Janet was a humble child of God and a very active member of the same church. I felt that there was some amount of love developing between Janet and me and seemingly growing steadily, but my spirit was restless, and my mind was sometimes unsettled as we talked to each other on a regular basis. I was on an uncertain path as I pondered over the possibility of an intimate relationship with Janet.

Janet has always been a very quiet and reserved person, one who exemplified the spirit of humility and grace. She was businesslike and jovial, but serious with God and her church activities, especially in matters of the youth department. She was competitive, hating to lose any competition held at church. She believed in winning at all times. Her standard was very high, and very few people could attain to that lofty height of self-satisfaction and team spirit. We maintained a close friendship, talking to each other, seeing each other on regular intervals, sharing thoughts and aspirations from time to time. However, we still did not verbalize our feelings for each other even though it was quite obvious that we loved each other. We were both shy individuals, who were brought up in similar Christian homes; therefore, we were not exposed to such auspicious prerogative as to the subject of *falling in love*.

After several weeks of contemplating on the subject of love, I decided to terminate my constant spirit of procrastination and venture upon the quest for a collective commitment toward cementing an intimate relationship with

Janet. I finally found enough courage to approach Janet and to make my intention known once and for all. So I requested an audience with her on the following Saturday after our regular sports day at the Titchfield High School grounds. She consented to meet with me later that day, not knowing what the subject matter on my mind was. Subsequently, the wonderful day of sport ended. I felt like springs were in my steps as I walked off the field of play, heading for my date with Janet. Soon, I met up with her and her closet friend, Thelma, on the road from Titchfield Hill, leading to the post office where they both worked and lived. We walked slowly down the steep hill. I felt like butterflies were in my chest—anxious, jubilant, yet apprehensive, not knowing how to begin and what to say. We finally reached her home. I sat alone on a chair in the living room for a while before Janet returned and sat directly before me. She too appeared apprehensive. She was nervous; and so was I, staring back at her for a few seconds, speechless. We had to be very discreet in our meeting since all eyes were usually on the young people of our church in everything we do and everywhere we go. So for me, I was taking a big chance in going to her house that summer evening, knowing that the possibility exist that by the next day, I could be reprimanded by my pastor and the elders of the church.

Janet was very anxious to hear what I had to say to her; she kept asking me, "What is it, Aubrey, that you want to talk about?" I was very shy and timid, not being exposed to the world of love before then, so I searched for the right word to utter. After staring at each other for a while, I finally told her that I was interested in an intimate relationship with her.

She smiled, covered her face in the palm of her hand for a few minutes, and then suddenly said, "I love you too." I was excited to hear this from her; now I felt a great release came over me. My heart felt strong, and my mind was at ease for the first time in a long time. It was a glorious day in my life as I departed her presence, dashing down the staircase of the city's central post office with a jubilant feeling of joy and contentment.

We continued on constant speaking terms on a regular basis, hoping to capitalize on the opportunity to cement a positive friendship that will eventually result in an eventual consolidation of an eternal intimacy. My instinct was leading toward making a serious commitment for the future with Janet, and even though our relationship was very young, I knew that courtship had its limits in the church teachings and doctrine; therefore, to prolong a relationship with the upper site—sex for more than six months would attract severe church detective surveillance in the form of the early church mothers whose password was "Shun the very appearance of evil." They had their Gospel gun out and were ready to fire at any cost, at any brother who seemed to walk or talk to any sister in the church.

Our friendship continued; we actually did not have a lot of time to meet with each other for more than one reason. Firstly, we were not allowed to be seen in public on a regular basis due to the strict adherence to the church Rules and regulations. Notwithstanding, I was somewhat uncertain of my position, thinking that perhaps other guys with a better economical and educational backgrounds may gain the edge over me as it related to Janet. On the other hand, my main concern was to be the thought of the "will of God" for my life. This was the watchword of Christianity and the solitary question of the believers in that sacred era. Above all, I wanted to be sure that I was in the perfect will of God in regard to my relationship with Janet.

In the pursuit for happiness and a constant communication with God, I prayed for direction in my daily endeavors. Fasting and prayer had been the main weapons of my Christian warfare as I sought God for His help in our relationship and a possible future together. There has always been a close relationship among the young people in the church over the years, and Janet and I were very much an integral part of that prestigious group at 52 West Street. Therefore, we had the opportunity to observe each other over a long period of time, which, of course, served as a great tool for personal assessment. Janet seemed to have developed a strong feeling toward me over a period of time, and the same could be said on my path; however, I had some amount of discernment that perhaps someday, this might not turn out the way we wanted it to be. But I could not put my finger on a particular reason at the time. So I went on living and loving, not knowing what the Master had in store for my life because it was only the perfect will of God that counted in those days of our lives.

We continued talking to each other on a daily basis, but in my spirit, I felt that I was losing her love; for what reason, I could not tell, but the feeling was strong enough to have caused me to ponder over it for several weeks. And perhaps those weeks turned into months. I tried very hard to remove the thoughts of insecurity from my mind, but each time, they came back forcefully to me. Now I was getting more and more concerned about the future of the relationship. Janet too was getting conscious of the fact that I was seeking a total commitment from her in regard to our relationship. However, I continued praying and fasting for God's direction concerning the situation, hoping that He will reveal Himself to me as to the path we should take into the future.

A few weeks later, Janet informed me that she had something to tell me. I was excited, yet apprehensive, not knowing what were the contents of her heart and which direction, if any, the relationship would take thereafter. I kept my heart open as I waited for the planned meeting with Janet at the city's central post office. There were moments when I felt that my heart was beating faster than it should, leading up to the time of the meeting. Anxious moments were fleeting away as I waited for that summer Saturday morning to arrive, and sure enough, it did. It was a planned sports day by the youth department of our church at the Titchfield High School, and everyone was out in their sports gear, ready to have a full day of fun. I was there in body, but my mind was on Janet and more so on what she wanted to tell me that was so important. I tried to play my natural game of cricket as usual, but I was clean bowled for a duck by a fast-moving delivery from my close friend, fast bowler David McFarlane of the Titchfield High School cricket team. I was definitely not concentrating on the game at hand, but rather on other things; so I lost my confidence at the batting crease and, ultimately, my mid stump that was uprooted by the fast moving ball.

As soon as the sports day was over, I dashed from the field, heading toward the post office with much anxiety. My mind was filled with lots of questions and was hoping to get some answers to them before the day was over. By the time I reached the post office, I saw Janet on the upstairs floor, looking out on the street; as soon as she laid eyes on me, she suddenly dashed down the long corridors, heading toward the dining room of the post office. I knew before that she was a very shy person, but this time, I suspected that something was about to happen for better or worse because I sensed it in my spirit from the moment I saw the look on her face from the bottom of the staircase and the way she ran down the alley with such a frantic expression left my troubled mind with added fear.

When I reached the dining room, I saw her best friend and co-worker, Thelma; she had I smile on her face, which told me something fishy was going on. And sure enough, Janet was not there. She had locked herself in her bedroom, afraid to come out and face me with what she had to tell me that day. I waited for about twenty minutes or more before she finally emerged from the bedroom, blushing, with her face covered with the palm of her hands. By this time, Thelma, knowing what was going on, discreetly left the scene; and Janet sat at the table across from me with her head down on the table, refusing to make any eye contact with me. I did not have a clue what she had in mind to share with me. I asked her repeatedly to let it out so that I will know what's in her heart, but she kept quiet, except for a few sobs every now and then. Then suddenly she looked up at me for the first time and said, "Do you really want to know what's in my heart, Aubrey?"

"Yes, my Janet," I replied. "That's what I am here for," I added. At that point, she began to explain everything to me concerning our relationship, how she felt about me and was hoping that our friendship would have turned into a great future; but there was someone else knocking at her heart's door, of which I was unaware off. And to add to the agony of my soul, she told me it was someone I knew very well, someone that was very close to me. She told me she was not going to tell me the name of the person because she did not want to hurt me further, but I was very persistent in finding out who was this person that had taken precedence over me.

Minutes and hours had passed by, and Janet was still adamant in keeping the secret from me forever. I began weeping uncontrollably like a baby. My heart was broken, my spirit sunk, my limbs went weak, and my mind began to wonder all over the place. Janet tried to comfort me, but to no avail. I was stunned out of my wit to hear such disappointing news, which was to mark the beginning and the end of a new saga in another chapter of my life as the burdens on my journey continued for yet another day. She informed me that, that "someone else" was knocking at her heart's door before me; therefore, she could not continue a relationship with me because it would not be fair to me and the other person. I appreciated her honesty and respected her for disclosing what was in her heart to me, but it hurts; my dreams were shattered and soon turned into nightmares before long. However, she showed great compassion, exercised maturity, and was very remorseful about the situation; and that I appreciated her for, even in that sad hour.

We have been in the relationship for a very short period of time, and this took me by surprise at a time when I was trying to capitalize on capturing her entire heart for good, not knowing that someone else has already taken that special spot in her heart. I did not want to lose someone that I loved, as I previously did, because of my passive attitude toward verbalizing my innermost feelings of intimacy that cost me the lost of another angel of Light. Sure enough, the days ahead were dark and dismal. I was living with a broken heart on the cutting edge of the twentieth century, not knowing if there was anyone on planet Earth to put the broken pieces back together again. So I turned to the one who knew all about sorrow, rejection, and broken hearts—the crucified Lord of Calvary. And He gave me peace in the midst of my storm and carried me on His shoulder of grace to a place of safety where under His wings I trusted securely from all harms.

On the other hand, Janet too was broken, caught between the present and the future; she had to make a choice, and so she did. I was left confused and uncertain about the future. I knew that it was the end of another chapter in my life. However, I insisted on her to tell me who that significant other was. I refused to leave her presence without getting an answer from her. I wanted to have a clear understanding that indeed the relationship was over, and from then, I would have known what path to take from that day forward. So she requested some more time to tell me who it was, but I was adamant in my quest to discover the unknown, not knowing what would be the outcome of that disclosure and what would be my reaction.

I was very curious to know who this person was, but she blatantly refused to tell me. So I waited patiently, persistently with inquiry; she was playing tough on me until finally, her heart broke when the tears came rolling down my cheeks. Her heart could no longer hold the secret; she had to get it out of her. She told me the person was one of my brothers. I began to smile through my tears, thinking that she was pulling my legs. But she said, "It's your elder brother, the one that lives in Kingston." When she said that, I paused for a moment, and you could hear a pin drop in the dining room; we both became silent as the night for almost ten minutes. My head hung low, and my spirit dropped within me. I was not angry, and I was not happy. There was no word suitable enough to describe my feeling, no song soothing enough to massage my pain away. I was caught in a conflict. I wanted to find the nearest exit out of the hall so that I could escape my feelings of rejection once and for all, but I could not move my feet from where it was lodged. Lifelessness came over me. I felt as if I was in a trance, dreaming of the next tomorrow and how I might rid myself of the burden of that unforgettable day.

This day of revelation took a hold on me for a while; and in the end, I wondered if I had done the right thing by forcing it out of her, only to discover that that someone was my own brother, Errol, who was then a policeman in the capital city. However, I knew I had to leave her presence, and perhaps for the last time, I struggled for a while before I could get to my feet and wondered if they were able to carry me out the door. Janet walked with me down the long corridors; it seemed endless as I dragged my weary feet upon the glittering tiles, perhaps for the last time. And there, my sad tale was recorded on the silent walls of history where the eternal truth of a damsel's heart was revealed. I bid her goodbye; this time, it was the finally one, from my heart to hers. Then I dashed for the open door, which led from upstairs to the main street of the city. My head was hanging low. I felt bitter, yet better—bitter because I was losing her, and better because she told me the truth before it was too late.

The relationship lasted for less than a year; I had walked away and picked up the broken pieces of my life. I must confess that for a while, I still felt some amount of love for Janet, and I knew that she was still in love with me; but we kept our Christian love and friendship without any ill feelings toward each other. I found help in God, who led me across that broken bridge into His green pasture of everlasting love. Nevertheless, life went on, and we remained good friends until this day. She subsequently married one of my close friends, Lloyd, and migrated to the United States of America shortly afterward.

After this experience, I drew closer to Christ, endeavoring to continue in the path of godliness. The church was blooming with young people; approximately 80 percent of the congregation consisted of female members as was the case in most churches on the island. In those days, we experienced great moments of unforgettable joy, mingled with some amount of burdens. The church grew rapidly on a weekly basis under the distinguished leadership of Rev. F. A. Beason. There was an unbroken bond of love among the young people at the Battle Factory Church. This contributed greatly in helping me to overcome my personal heartbreak as my burdens gradually subsided for a period of time.

I was at the end of my recovery from a broken heart; my mind was on the kingdom of God, awaiting the return of the Messiah. My eyes had seen the glory of His coming, and I yearned for the heavenly city, the New Jerusalem. I tried to forget the past by drowning myself in spiritual things with a view to rid my soul of that sad Saturday. The years went by, slowly, I cried a river of tears, trying to wash memories of Janet away.

In the year 1978 as it drew near to the closing of the winter season, soldiers from the island of Bermuda were visiting Jamaica. They camped at Mitchell's Folly, near the seacoast town of Port Antonio. Among the military personnel were born-again Christians from the church of God in Bermuda. These men sought a place to worship and found a branch of their church, the New Testament Church of God (Battle Factory Church) at 52 West Street. They were under the command of Sergeant Glen Braham, a doctor in the Bermudan army; he was also a brilliant Gospel singer and an anointed preacher. During our family training hour (F.T.H) service, four burly military officers walked into the church and were escorted by an usher unto the rostrum where our pastor, Rev. F. A. Beason, gave them a hearty welcome and seated them. All eyes were fixed on the soldiers dressed in military outfit. The choir song beautifully; they cheered and worshipped as we do. Suddenly, it dawned on me that these men ought to be Christians from the way they worshipped God.

Soon, it was time for the pastor to take his stance and make his formal introduction; the excited congregants listened and watched. The pastor introduced them one by one, explaining their various ranks in the military. He told us where they were from and their purpose in the country and how they took time out to worship at our church. The people cheered with great joy; then our pastor invited Dr. Glen Braham to the microphone. He gave a powerful testimony of how God saved him from the things he used to do on his previous trips to Jamaica; then he sang, "Thanks to Calvary, I am not the boy I used to be. Thanks to Calvary, things are different than before." The vast congregation gave him a standing ovation as the Spirit of God moved upon the audience with much force. The singing sergeant was joined by another sergeant and two corporals; now it was a soldiers' quartette. As they struck the first note, the audience became spellbound; everyone was on their feet. The church was charged with spiritual excitement after the soldiers sang, "His eyes are on the sparrow, and I know He watches over me." The Holy Spirit was evident in the church; after they sang a number of songs, Sergeant

Braham began to preach. Suddenly, three visitors slipped into the back row of the church; among them were a detective sergeant of the police, a hotel storeroom manager, and an airline customer service supervisor.

These three visitors were passing the church and heard the melodious voices and were led by the Spirit of God inside the church. They were on their way to a nightclub, but God must have directed them to the church. While the soldier was preaching, they listened and watched with eagerness. The preacher clad in a military outfit brought an unusual aura to the pulpit; this was very strange to most of us. The fascination was obvious, and the fact that he took time out from the military camp to share the Gospel to the church inspired the believers further in their quest for more of God.

During the sermon, the airline supervisor was convicted by the Spirit of God. She tried to hide her convicted feelings from her friends, but the tears kept rolling down her beautiful cheeks like a river coming down a hill. After the sermon, an invitation was given for those who need Christ to come to the altar; the airline supervisor, Elecia Patterson, was the first person to reach the altar. She cried to God in sincere repentance; her sins were forgiven, and she accepted the Lord Jesus Christ as her personal savior. Her life was completely transformed by the Holy Spirit. Her two friends were witnesses to this miraculous event. Salvation came to her, and the joy of the Lord became her strength from thereafter. She found a new experience and had a changed heart and a clear conscience that evening of divine intervention.

Her friends kept their cool until after the service, and then they started joking around about Elecia's decision to go to the altar. For them, it was a joke; but by now, Elecia was sweetly saved by the power of the Gospel preached by that Bermudian soldier. She had experienced a supernatural visitation from God, one that changed the course of her life forever. Soon, news of her conversion to Christianity spread near and far; some rejoiced with her while others were skeptical, doubting that she could ever become a Christian. One of her coworkers, airport manager George Hannah exclaimed, "If Elecia is converted, then there is a God!" During this era, a host of people came to Christ as Elecia's conversion was noised abroad. She held strong to her newfound faith, assembling with the saints at West Street on a regular basis. This she found joy in doing as her relationship grew rapidly with the Lord and the church folks. It was a new experience for her; so she had to learn the rules, doctrines, and regulations of the church, which was mandatory for all new converts. However, she was not afraid to venture upon new thoughts and ideologies in order to deepen her faith in the things of God.

The weeks and months that followed were characterized with many conversions in her family, and revival broke out at 52 West Street. Her conversion became the capstone to this revival in the city, which brought many critics to her baptismal service to witness that history-making event. On the day of her baptism, a massive crowd gathered at Bryan's Bay to witness the event. It was absolute pandemonium at Bryan's Bay that afternoon of February when people from all walks of life came to see Elecia immersed into the water by the Reverend Fedlyn A. Beason. There were traffic congestions on the roads that led to Bryan's Bay. People came on foot, on bicycles, motorbikes, cars, buses, and donkeys to the baptismal service. A helicopter flew low overhead with a view to capture the majestic scenery of the baptism on camera.

Elecia's conversion made headlines, and so was her baptismal service; she was well-known in the community, so news of her change of lifestyle attracted many onlookers to her side for many weeks and months that followed. Her conversion was that of a soldier's story; she was led to Christ by a soldier who told the story of Jesus, who championed the cause of humanity to bring freedom to a world of sin and shame. That story still resonates with her today, how a soldier brought to her heart's door the gift of salvation, which changed the course of her life for eternity. From that night forward, she went on her way, rejoicing in the god of her salvation, spreading the good news of her newfound experience to family, friends, and enemies alike without fear. She was fulfilling the great commission in her own way in the ministry of personal evangelism and the sharing of her testimony. In doing this, she began to create an impact on her coworkers, her family, the church, and the community in general as her influence led others to believe in the Christian way of life.

I too was influenced by the soldiers who ministered to the people of God that night and more so to me in particular. My argument was that God had heard the prayer of my heart and delivered me from the agony of a broken relationship. In those sacred days of Sundry times, the main emphasis at church was placed on *receiving the baptism of the Holy Spirit.*

As young people, we had a passion for the things of God, and there was a spiritual fire burning in our bosoms as we sought after godliness and holiness. Prayer and the study of the scriptures were a part of the daily routine for the saints of that church era.

A few months after the soldiers left town, the newly converted sister, Elecia Patterson, had a heavenly visitation in the person of the Holy Spirit while she was on the job at the Ken Jones Airport. She felt the presence of the Lord while she was checking in the passengers for the next flight. Later, she took a break; and while walking slowly toward an abundant aircraft, she began to feel the quickening power of the Holy Spirit. She was on fasting that day, determined to be filled with the Spirit and to get closer to God; and sure enough, God granted the desire of her heart. She began to pray as she approached that old aircraft, and then something unusual happened that day; she began to speak a new language, one she had not learned from a classroom or from a book, but it was a heavenly language—it was the *baptism of the Holy Spirit*. She was scared, knowing that she was on the job, not wanting her coworkers to see her in the Spirit, knowing that they would have no understand hearing her speaking in other language. However, she rejoiced in the fact that God had answered her prayer and granted her request.

As for me, my mind was fixed on heaven, and my heart was in the avenue of the god of love, with no intention to travel down an intimate path for any time soon. My first exchange of words with Elecia was very brief, yet interestingly captivating. My heart burned within me that Thursday's eve, when my love for her began to sneeze. And even though I was apprehensive in traveling down that route where love abode, there was a sense of feeling within me that we were knocking on each other's heart's door with a sense of uncovered importunity. It was on that beautiful Thursday night that I first laid eyes on Elecia as she stood, looking at me through the side window of the church. Something moved within me as she stared at me with a passion and a smile that lit up my dark night and brought sunshine on those cloudy hours of my past days.

I had no intention of falling in love with her, but it seemed to be love at first sight, love that would not let me go. I sought the Lord in dealing with those strong feelings toward Elecia that seemed to haunt me like a ghost. The more I prayed to get rid of those feelings, the more my love grew toward her. I was getting very concerned about this new development in my life, knowing that I wanted to stay clear of any relationship at least for a while. During church services, we often made eye contact with each other but did not exchange any words at all. I had a strong feeling that we would somehow become close friends later, but I was keeping my eyes on Christ alone, not thinking about earthly matters because my eyes were fixed on heaven.

Honestly, I was a very shy person; so for the most part, I avoided having any conversation with Elecia. And even though I wanted her friendship, there was no effort on my path to converse with her. However, after a while, the nonverbal communication became very intense, on both sides, as we would sit on opposite sides of the aisle of the church each Sunday. During this period, I wrote several articles in the leading national newspaper, the *Gleaner*, and was writing a series of poetry, short stories, and plays for the church's drama group. It was then that I developed the idea of writing about my struggles. So I began writing the first chapter of this book when she captured my heart in the season of spring. There were times when I tried to resist my feelings of love for Elecia, but they were stronger than I had anticipated. My greatest concern was about the will of God for my life.

The fact that she was new in the Body of Christ brought some amount of concern to me as I pondered about a possible relationship with her. However, her positive attitude, hospitable personality, and captivating smile dispelled all doubts and fear from my mind and drove my heart closer to her. By now, my love for her began to expand to a greater dimension; and soon, I was deeply in love with her. I tried to resist looking at her at church, avoiding any form of conversation where possible, but nothing seemed to work in my favor. She too had a big crush on me even though she too was trying to hide her feelings toward me.

Soon, she found out that I was doing some writing and needed a typist, so she volunteered to assist me to this end. By this time, she had no idea that I was falling in love with her. She approached me and offered her service to type the story I was working on entitled "The Early Days of My Childhood." After she typed the first portion of the story, I reviewed it and concluded that her typing was very impressive. In addition to this, she informed me that she would avail herself to type any work that I might have now and in the future. I was elated when she spoke to me and expressed her desire to assist me on this project. This, of course, opened the opportunity for me to have dialogue with Elecia concerning my intimate feelings for her.

My love for Elecia continued to grow rapidly like a fertilized plant in the season of spring. I could not keep this spontaneous feeling of love in me for long. My spirit yearned for her love like parched ground in desert land. I longed for the raindrops of sweet words from her lips and for the moment to come when I would have poured out my heart into hers, but it seemed like time was a thousand years out of my reach. However, I waited and waited for that glorious unknown day when God would grant me strength, wisdom, and courage to venture upon that glad tomorrow when I would have unveiled the secret of my innermost being to the girl of my dreams. I was timid and shy and could not tell why, perhaps clustered by the broken dreams of yesteryears or too excited about the present experience of *falling in love* to utter the phrase "I love you" to another.

The moment finally came like sunshine on a cloudy day. It was Sunday, April 28, 1978; the powerful Spirit-filled youth Sunday morning's service ended about 1:30 p.m. Elecia extended an invitation to some of the church folks to have dinner at her house as she often did ever since she became a Christian. The invitation was open especially to those who were living a far distance from church. She felt this was her way of doing well for others, and most importantly, she wanted to be close to the matured, experienced believers because she was eager to learn more about God and the church. She gave me a personal invitation to join the group for dinner that Sunday evening. My heart was filled with joy, knowing this was the chance of a lifetime to reveal the secret of my heart to her. On the other hand, fear and doubt took a hold of me, and my knees began to shake like feeble men at war. I was scared, yet elated, not knowing how to approach her and to express my feelings for her or what her respond to me would be.

However, after the service, we all walked slowly up the town; some were conversing about the great service we had while others just strolled quietly toward Elecia's house at Plymouth Hill. Elecia and I walked slowly behind, having a nice chat, mostly about the day's service. I said in my heart this was the perfect opportunity for me to tell her how I felt about her, but I got cold feet; and even though the words were at the tip of my tongue, I did not utter a word to her on that subject matter. Upon reaching home, I was immediately introduced to her family members; unfortunately, I did not meet her mom as she was living in the United States of America. However, I met the rest of the family who were living with her at the time, including Dorett, Janet, Joy, Lloyd, and Joy's daughter, Keris, and Auntie

Maize. They all extended a warm welcome to me on that beautiful evening of brilliant sunshine. Although the temperature was in the nineties, I had cold feet. This was my day, the greatest chance of a lifetime to express my feeling of love, but fear and doubt kept coming down the corner of my mind. I kept staring at Elecia, speechless. It seemed like my world was turning upside down as a thousand thoughts flashed down the center of my love-struck mind.

Then suddenly, she looked across from where I was sitting and smiled; my life was lit up with a ray of hope that broke the frantic tension of my being, which held me hostage for a while. It was at this point that I knew the floor was open for something out of the ordinary. I smiled back at her and gestured in a nonverbal manner, and somehow, she knew there was something on my mind. She drew near to where I sat and reclined in the settee beside me; then out from my trembling lips flew these unforgettable words as I softly whispered, "Elecia, I have something to tell you."

"Me too," she replied. I wondered what on earth she wanted to tell me. She was very excited and was anxious to hear what I had to say to her. I had not the slightest idea what was on her mind. As far as I was concerned, I was on the verge of ruining her day, revealing that I was in love with her. This brought some amount of concern to me as I pondered over the fact that she was new in the Christian pathway, and I was bound by duty to help her to find the path to heaven.

She kept urging me consistently to disclose the secret of my heart to her before dinnertime, but the words I wanted to say could not come out as fast as I planned. So I promised to tell her later; she consented to this because dinner was now ready, and the other folks called us to the table. She requested a seat beside me at the table. This made me even more nervous, knowing that I was in the company of some of the greatest defenders of the faith, who could see through a concrete wall in the Spirit; therefore, I was afraid that they would, through the Spirit of discernment, see the contents of my heart what I was about to share with Elecia after dinner. My experience told me that this was possible, seeing that I had the same *gift of discernment* like some of the other folk present at the table. By this time, Elecia was discreetly appealing to my emotion at the dinner table for me to give her a hint of what was on my mind. The way she stared at me told me that she knew exactly what I was going to say that evening.

There was an intense connection between her and me while we sat at that table of fine dining in the presence of some of the most precious people on earth.

This, of course, gave me some amount of confidence, courage, and expectation as I anticipated a warm reception into her heart of love. Notwithstanding, her body language spoke clearly that the first day of the rest of our lives was about to commence on that unforgettable evening of intimate disclosure. When dinner ended, excitement was floating down the streams of my heart like never before. Elecia too had her moment of enthusiastic expectations as she quickly cleared the dinner plates from the table and returned to the living area where I was sitting. Without uttering a word, she looked me straight in the eyes. I blushed, turned my head, and smiled. "Do you want to hear what I have to say now?" I asked Elecia.

"Sure! Sure!" she replied.

I told her I will tell her at a later date, but she would have none of it; she wanted to hear it right at that moment and not another. After a brief pause, I looked at her and said, "I will tell you later." She insisted she wanted to hear on that same hour and not a minute later. I was so shy, I wanted to run for the door, but she kept me at bay. Then finally, I found some courage and strength, so I told her to go into the other room and pick up the extension telephone; then I would tell her what was in my heart. I was too shy to tell her face-to-face that I was in love with her. She ran into the room and grabbed the telephone receiver with excitement, and then I whispered quietly in a soft tone, "I am in love with you."

After hearing these words, she returned quickly to the living room where I was sitting; she covered her face in the palm of her hands, blushing like a little girl, and said, "I have something to tell you too." Then she exclaimed, "Brother Brown, I must confess that *I love you very much*. I have been admiring you for some time now." She added this childishly as she dashed out of the living room into her bedroom and locked the door.

My heart began to palpitate faster than before. I felt a sense of release as I sat on the settee in complete wonderment. After about half an hour, she returned to the living room and sat down without saying a word; she looked at me, and I looked at her. This went on for about ten minutes; then I said, "I really love you"

She replied, "I love you too." She told me, "Let's pray about this."

I replied, "Why not now?" We began to pray, and soon, our voices echoed across the room so that some of the other folks heard us praying and joined us. Then soon, it turned into a prayer meeting at Plymouth Hill that spread to the neighbor's house, who came rushing down the alley to join us in prayer. The prayer session went on for a while; it was getting closer to church time; so we ended the prayer meeting, got ready, and left for church at 52 West Street.

It was an evening of unforgettable memories of intimate confessions when Elecia and I poured out our hearts to each other on that fair hour of godly and human excitement, which marked out the mountain tracks that led to the paths of a future forever. When I knew the feeling was neutral between Elecia and me, it brought joy to my ears and gradually vanished my midnights of fear and shyness away. She had been my secret admirer for a while, and upon this confession of love, my eyes began to look toward the golden hills of that glad tomorrow when at last she'll say "I do." Then I will wrap my arms around her delightful frame and ask her, if she would be my future bride. It was at this point that I revealed to Elecia that I had written to her mom in Ohio, U.SA to ask her for her daughter's hand in marriage. Elecia was astonished when she learned that I was in touch with her mom, whom I had never met, she had no clue that I even knew her address, but I obtained it from her brother, Lloyd. She was impressed with the fact that I went to that level of dignity to ask her mom for her daughter in marriage and never cease to mention this to others when reflecting on the day I walked into her life and change it forever.

As we left for church that evening, Elecia and I walked together; the others strolled on before us. I asked her if there was a chance for us in the future; she replied, "Let's pray and think about it seriously." Now my heart was enlarged by the contagious spirit of love that touched every fiber of my being and put springs in my steps. This love was stronger than death and endless like eternity. We began our journey of love from that day forward into the unknown, not knowing what the future held, but depended on God's grace to lead us along. Our relationship became more and more serious as the days and weeks went by; our love for each other was growing faster than we could count the passing days. There was an amazing clarity and understanding between us as the months progressed, and we knew then that we were meant for each other.

Our golden days of courtship began; we were filled with excitement and great assurance. There was a tremendous amount of respect, love, and adoration for each other. On the other hand, it was very difficult for Elecia and me to communicate as often as we would like to due to the religious restrictions of our day. Our relationship was always under the scrutiny of the elders of the church and the public in general. It was the common teachings and practice of the early church to apply very strict rules and regulations to those who were in courtship. We were not free to walk side by side in public places, and if we were frequently seen together, we would be strongly reprimanded by the church elders. In those days of my early Christian life, the church was extremely strict to the point where I felt like I was committing a serious crime because I fell in love with Elecia.

Shortly after Elecia and I had revealed our love for each other, we discovered that the road ahead was not going to be an easy one. Therefore, divine help was urgently needed to chart the course of our lives from there onward. Indeed, *burdens were on my journey*. I had fallen in love, but now it was the test of my life to see if my life was going to fall apart. However, I was determined to go over and not under the raging tides of life's struggles. Being conscious of God's righteousness, I was guided by the gifted, anointed man of God in the person of my pastor, Rev. F.A. Beason, who was nicknamed FAB from the television advertisement of a laundry detergent entitled Fab Wash White and Clean. This was associated with this preacher as a result of his nature of conducting the business of God and the church and his constant emphasis on living a clean Christian lifestyle.

The fear of a holy god was constantly upon my life. When Rev. Beason preached, you would feel the presence of God among men. Never had I seen a man so gifted in the exposition of God's Word and the administration of the Battle Factory Church. He was at the zenith of his ministry, and he brought the church to the pinnacle of its spirituality. Therefore, those who grew up under his ministry became candidates for heaven in the midst of satanic assaults. As a result of these factors, my spiritual belt was guarded, my faith became stronger, and my face was turned toward the portals of glory. However, beneath the heavenly vision was a heavy burden that was threatening to tear my soul apart. The conflicts escalated, and oppositions increased rapidly against our intimate relationship; my frantic frame began to tremble, my sorrow multiplied, and it felt like the enemy was tearing the heart right out of me. Some of my own church folks turned against me when they learned I was in love with Elecia; some criticized, and others began to backbite and devour me with mean and callous indignities. My life had become the main headline of the day, the center of attraction, and the talk of the town. I was on a rocky road on a trip to the unknown path of love, not knowing what was going to befall me; the devil wanted me dead or alive, but all I was guilty of was *falling in love*, and this was the crime of my day on the pilgrim's journey.

There were times I was lied on, literally confronted by my brethren, tried by my elders, and reprimanded by my pastor. To add fire to fury, my own family members got involved in the tantalizing scenario of my personal love affair. Now my world was turning faster than it should and my nights darker than usual, my food turned water in my mouth, and my pants waist was getting slack. I was in a crisis, and no one was near except Jehovah God. The earthly friends were few, including Brother Balford, (Trucky) Curtis, his mom, Sister Mary Curtis, and his nephew, Brother Othniel (Scopy) Watson, and Sister Sharon Brown. These wonderful comforters cheered my soul while coming home from church each night, with a word or two to take me through the night. Some of my relatives were opposed to the relationship for one reason or another; some voiced their objections while others silently remained neutral. A vast number of the young people in our church became restless; some were adamant in their quest to destroy any possible glimpse of matrimonial intentions.

There were many beautiful girls in the church who loved and admired me greatly; some even had high hopes that I would ask their hands in marriage one day. Then there were those who felt that they were losing that glorious hope and opportunity; therefore, they were determined to banish the relationship between Elecia and me by whatever means necessary. We were scared as could be, finding ourselves in an unusually dangerous territory where the darts of Satan were coming from all angles simultaneously, desiring to close this exciting and frantic chapter of our lives. But like the Apostle Paul, the converted persecutor of Tar- shish, we were persuaded that "nothing shall be able to separate us from the love of God, which is in Christ Jesus" and, subsequently, the love for each other that we so seriously cherished. Despite the testing of our faith, we remained true to God and to each other. We had our eyes set on holiness as we sought God in prayer and fasting on a weekly basis. This was the key to deliverance as were thought by some of the older folks in church.

And so we needed deliverance, badly, and more so that God's divine will be worked out in our lives.

Although the battles were hard to fight and the conflicts seemed unbearable, we proceeded with much anticipation that one day soon our love for each other will blossom into something eternal. We suffered many persecutions and atrocities from our own church folks. There were bitter days, seemingly endless encounters with opposing folks from all over the city in which we lived and beyond. Folks from all over began to speculate and criticize our relationship in a hostile and negative way and, in the process, were putting enormous strains on our relationship and ultimately on our Christianity. There were undesirable comments about us, misleading reports, personal attacks, and collective disagreements. In all these unbearable trials and tests, we remained steadfast in love; it seemed like nothing could detour us from the sacred path of an endless love in the midst of the most agonizing struggles of life's tempestuous journey.

On the other hand, nothing seemed to detour the onslaughts of the objectors as they lay in wait for another attack at our integrity. In the meantime, Elecia and I were persuaded in our hearts that God was in our relationship and that we were heading in the right direction to the place where love abode. However, others felt differently, so they began to express their feelings of dissatisfaction concerning our relationship without reservation. As the persecution intensified, news of our relationship spread wide and far throughout the nation and even to foreign countries. By this time, we have made headline in Satan's leading newspaper, and many of its readers began to pass their own judgment upon us and expressed their desire to destroy the relationship by whatever means. Some of my close brethren forsook me; others jumped on the bandwagon to join in the growing movement for disruption. They attacked my character like hungry lions prancing on their prey. It was then that I thought *what an awful price to pay for the crime of falling in love.*

One thing I knew for sure, I was blessed with tolerance and faith in God, which sustained my finite being on the edge of the unexpected storms of life. I could depend upon the old mothers of Zion and the fathers of the faith for their words of wisdom, encouragement, and prayers. However, those determined objectors of our courtship had sleepless nights, making plans to dismantle my love for Elecia Patterson; but my love for her was strong as death and endless like eternity. For this purpose, I was lied on, buffeted, mistrusted, forsaken, stoned, and rejected by my own countrymen. I was prohibited from taking active part in church services, brought before the elders, reprimanded by my pastor, and verbally assaulted by some of my kinfolks. Perhaps some had my best interest at heart but went the wrong way in expressing it to me. I thought to myself, *there has to be a more excellent way in giving council to a brother that was truly in love. But* to me *they choose the wrong methods to voice their opinions about our relationship.*

There were times when I felt I had lost my freedom of worship in a church that was so conducive to such atmosphere, more than any other I had known over these years. It was a tremendous struggle for me to sit in the company of those who despised me the most. And even though I was possessed with humility, it was an uphill task to stabilize the burdens of my heart and to rid myself of such enormous discomforts in my beloved church. I had no other alternatives but to seek for divine help in dealing with the numerous seemingly unending burdens of my soul. Therefore, I prayed—perhaps more than I ever prayed before, with a quest to rid myself of this agonizing sorrow and the burdens of my fainting heart that came upon me without warning.

Even in those sad hours, there was hope and faith that these troublesome moments will one day turn to a glad tomorrow. I had a great confidence in my heart that Elecia was the one for me, so my love for her grew fonder, with a foreseeable future that seemed bright and blessed. It was during this period of our courtship that Elecia introduced me to the famous Frenchman's Cove Hotel training school and, subsequently, to the training manager, Mr. Samuel Campbell, and the general manager, Mr. Frank Lawrence. I immediately took up the challenge to enroll in the one-year training course at the hotel training school with a view to become a formal dining room waiter. The training manager was very thorough, strict, and disciplined. He was a man with a tremendous amount of experience in the hospitality business; and there was no letting up in his deliberations as he sought to bring out the best in all of us at the training school, situated on the magnificent lush, salubrious property on the brink of the Caribbean Ocean in San San Bay, Portland, Jamaica.

After the course ended, I was immediately employed to the hotel as a formal dining room waiter. This was a chance of a lifetime to work in such a prestigious historic hotel visited by famous guests such as Errol Flynn, John Wayne, Ronald Reagan, prime ministers, and other famous movie stars. This was my first taste of the hospitality industry and I loved every moment of it. Unfortunately, after working for a year at the Frenchman's Cove Hotel, the hotel was in the process of closing or changing management; so I decided to seek another employment at the historic Bonnie View Plantation Hotel, located on a twenty-two-acre property, six hundred feet above sea level. This meant I was going to be working closer to home and at a more viable tourist destination. It was the peak of the winter season when I arrived at my new job; therefore, I knew that I was going to cash in on the opportunity to make some big bucks. Sure enough, it turned out well for me financially.

Two years went by quickly in my new job where I found favor in the boss's eyes and was treated well. At that time, my Christian life was on a spiritual high; and I soon led the general manager's wife, Mrs. Myrtle Weetom, to the Lord Jesus Christ on the hotel's property. Mrs. Weetom was a Chinese woman coming out of a predominantly Roman Catholic Church background, but the Lord allowed her to find favor with me, and this gave me the opportunity to tell her about the saving grace of Jesus Christ. She had never met Jesus as her personal savior; but that day, when I led her to the Lord, she wept bitterly while we sat under the cashew tree on the hotel's property. She confessed to me that she was planning to take her own life the same day I led her to Christ.

Soon, Mrs. Weetom and I became prayer partners as we would join in prayer every morning under the cashew tree, behind the kitchen, to pray for her strength in the Lord. She was fearful of coming to my church, knowing that her entire family was Roman Catholic and perhaps would ultimately abandoned her; but I worked vigorously with her, giving her the assurance that Christ will never leave her nor forsake her. After a few weeks of prayers, counseling, and persuasion, she decided to visit my church at 52 West Street. I took her to the church the next Sunday morning with the permission of her husband, Mr. Bertram Weetom, Pro, as he was affectionately called by the staff. She was very impressed with our way of worship and decided she wanted to come back the next week.

After the second visit to our church, Mrs. Weetom was totally convinced that God had a hand in her life, so she decided that the Battle Factory Church at 52 West Street was going to be her place of worship. The grace of God was upon her, and one could tell that her life was changed because of the new joy on her face since she found the Lord. She started attending the new convert's class and was later baptized and received into the fellowship of the church of God. My heart rejoiced that night when she was immersed into the water at the baptismal pool; the service was rich and powerful as the people of God shouted for joy when they saw for the first time a Chinese woman becoming a member of the church, especially one of such lofty strata of the society. This, no doubt, allowed us to understand that God was no respecter of persons. He calls whomsoever He will.

Mrs. Weetom's conversion to Christianity had left me excited and more determined to serve the Lord despite of the agony of my burdens and the constant threats of the enemy to destroy my love for Elecia. In my heart, there was a renewed sense of hope that one day; she would say I do, despite the negative attacks on our relationship. I knew that she was madly in love with me, yet uncertain about a future together because of the various criticisms from folks in regard to the relationship. To add to this agony was the fact that some of the criticisms were coming from those who were close relatives and friends that were dear to us. Despite of this testing period, I was willing to go on record at any moment to make an official proposal for marriage to Elecia, the one I loved so dear; but in the meantime, she was making her intentions known to all to depart the shores of Jamaica to the United State of America. She was fed up of the criticisms, gossips, heresies, and struggles that surrounded the relationship and the constant trials and persecutions she had to bear because of her love for me. As far as she was concerned, the time had come to depart that scene to another; she had had enough of church folks and was changing her location once and for all.

The night she told me of her planned departure, my heart felt like it was broken into a thousand pieces that could not be put back together again. She added to my sorrow when she said, "Aubrey, our relationship is over. I want to close this chapter of my life and leave Jamaica for good." My heart began to race frantically. I cried like a baby and persuaded her to stay, but her mind was already made up, and her decision was final. Nothing I say could change her heart about leaving her homeland and the one she loved and adored. She left me standing in the distance with a broken heart as she walked away from my presence. For me, that night was the darkest one on planet Earth; my earnest expectation was terminated, and my radiant world was turned upside down. Sadness and sorrow filled my thoughts in the days leading up to her departure. I had sleepless nights and broken dreams as I pondered in my heart, *Why, Lord?* I waited for an answer from above, but it seemed hopeless. I was left with pain and sorrow, thinking of the next tomorrow that would bring the darkness when she finally departed. She was my future bride, but in a few short days, I was about to lose that lively hope that she would be a part of me. A thousand thoughts came crashing down the memory of my life. I saw dark clouds on a sunny day and black nights when the moon was full. I wished the nights never fell nor the mornings ever broke. I felt empty, helpless, and lost at church, at home, and on the job. I was affected, rejected, and dejected. In a vast city of humankind, I was yet among others, but was lost in love; no one else knew my heart, except the one above. Loneliness, no rest, and I condescended to strangers and felt as if I was at my end.

The next Sunday morning the church Public relations officer announced Elecia's departure, and as usual a special send-off service was held in her honor. She was an ardent worker in the kingdoms; therefore, her service to God and the church was appreciated. And now that she was leaving, there were many church folks grieving. I sat quietly in that sorrowful service, thinking of all the struggles Elecia and I had gone through during our time of courtship. I knew that she was meant for me, and now that she was leaving, it tore my heart right out of me. Now the hour was coming fast when the *girl of my dreams* would be suddenly wrenched out of my hand and perhaps land into that of another. I was there to hear her say goodbye in such untimely manner. My heart ached with intense pain; I could not have held back the flowing tears from my weeping eyes and the obvious agony of my brokenhearted soul. My world was falling apart; my dreams suddenly turned into nightmares as I pondered over my uncertain future. A multitude of thoughts flashed across my mind as the solemn service continued. I began to reminisce on our limited time spent together since we first met, and those precious thoughts tore my heart in many pieces.

At that farewell function, Elecia was decked in her glamorous outfit. Many speeches were given by representatives of the various departments of the church. There were musical selections from well-wishers who came to bid her farewell. It was a very moving occasion for everyone present, knowing that she was a very popular, well-respected person in the community. There were special singing and commendation from a wide cross section of the city and from the saints at Battle Factory Church. I listened and watched in disbelief, wondering if I was dreaming, but to Elecia this was real. She was leaving the country for good; and that was my final hour to capture the moment of a lifetime, the departure of the *girl of my dreams*, and to behold her beauty and charm for perhaps the last time in my life.

Elecia received many gifts and flowers from her well-wishers; among those gifts was one from my heart to hers—a poem I wrote, typed, and framed in fine stained wood entitled "When You're Gone." It was written as a tribute to my love, an expression of a brokenhearted man. It turned out that this poem was the golden piece of writing that changed Elecia's life and mine from that year to all the others that followed. The evening of great memories ended with hugs, weeping, sighing, and sadness as the elegant hometown girl took her final salute from the people of that sacred city of ours in which she has lived since the day of her birth. Now she was departing with tears, leaving her loved ones behind, not knowing what tomorrow would bring. I wished her Godspeed, with a hug, and whispered in her ears sweet words of love from the passion of my heart. I told her, "Let's elope and get marry abroad."

She replied sarcastically, "Have a safe flight and a happy landing." A cloud of sorrow came over me as she uttered those words. I wanted to find an uninhabited place to accommodate my feelings of utmost rejection by the one I adored, and now that she was leaving, I felt a final nail was driven into the center of my heart that could rend the life right out of me. From there, I thought this was the final attempt to express my love for her, and there she turned my ray of hope into despair when she blatantly desecrated my desperate attempt to change her mind from leaving her glorious home and me behind with a broken heart.

When You're Gone
In sorrow, I'll be
When thou shall be gone,
Then darkness over me
Shall surely be born,
Hope to meet with thee
On that early morn,
When gladly, you I'll see.

I shall take my rest
When you shall be gone
In my lonely nest,
I shall have no warm
I may lose my best,
My sorrow brings harm
Thy love, I request.

In tears, you will depart
Don't love another guy
You will break my heart,
My sorrow shall multiply
When you go up north
I will have to cry,
And I will be wroth.

When you shall be gone
At that uncertain hour,
This agony will make alarm
Love will have more power
There will be no calm
On my lonely tower,
I will be all forlorn.

Doubtful shall I be
When you're far across
The ocean, away from me,
Hoping our paths to cross
When again, I shall meet thee,
On that green, green grass
When at last, my love I'll see.

In dismay, shall I live?
Perhaps I will have to die
If thy love to another give,
Surely, I'll have to cry
I'm yours forever to be
Love thee, can't tell why,
Oh dear! Don't hurt me.

When you shall be gone
I won't sleep in the night,
Nor greet the early morn
Until I know you'll be all right,
When you shall be gone
Oh dear! Remember me, my light,
My love of daylight dawn.

These were the words that came from my heart as I penned them upon common parchment to the girl of my dreams, Elecia Patterson—the one I loved the one I adored. I was a drowning man so deeply sunk in love. I was desperately holding on to a straw that would perhaps bring hope to my fainting spirit of brokenness and pain. Then of course, not being able to venture into the unknown, I was hoping and dreaming that the poetry written by the trembling feeble fingers of a brokenhearted guy would change the heart of such illustrious fathom of delight to return to fulfill her godly vows upon that golden shore of sweet romance.

A few days later, Elecia left the shores of our homeland and bid her loved ones farewell with the hope to meet again. But as for me, it was the end. Oh, how my heart bled with bitter tears of unforgettable memories of the girl of my dreams who I hoped would become my wife. Somehow, within me, I had this hidden hope that it was not over as she said; but I trusted in God that he would see me through. I knew God had a plan and purpose for me, and I felt strongly that all was not lost because once there was life, I had hope that God would come through for me. I felt in my heart that one day, Elecia would come back to me, and we would be together forever. There was a silver lining in my dark dungeon of despair that told me there was a bright light on the other side of midnight. So I held on to a glimpse of hope that one day, she will think it over and renew our relationship. From Elecia's point of view, she was through with the relationship; as for me, I was holding on to anything I could find so as not to lose the hope of her returning.

When she left for America, I still kept that close bond with her sisters and brothers. I would visit them and inquire about Elecia. I felt like my world had fallen apart. A part of my life was missing. I felt lonely, dejected, and lost without her. The days and the nights seemed longer than before; my mind wandered from home to distant land as I searched for Elecia in my dreams. Her pleasant face kept rolling down the corner of my mind as I tried to wash her memories away with uncontrollable tears. What hurt me most was the fact I had no way of communicating with her, seeing that she had already told me that the relationship was over. Therefore, she refused to give me any information concerning her whereabouts. Prior to her departure, I once asked her to marry me before she left town or wait for me when she got to America, and I'd meet her there so that we could get married. Her reply was not a positive one, so I knew then that she had made up her mind that it was over between us.

Somehow, I had this crazy idea that it was not over until God said so. I had a certain amount of confidence that it was the will of God for Elecia and me to be married one day, and I was determined not to go down without a fight, so I held on to an inner feeling that told me there was going to be a new tomorrow and that I would see my baby again. Her folks could not always understand the confidence that I spoke with then, believing that Elecia will one day return and marry me. But I believed there was a higher power that possessed me and gave me the assurance in my time of great sorrow and pain. So I went on praying and hoping for the best in my worst days.

It was now eight days since Elecia left, but to me, it seemed like a hundred years had gone by. The proceeding days brought much pain and agony to my life and probably filled my life with more than I could bear to the point where I had to seek council from God and my pastor in this matter. As I continued steadfast in my Christian walk, attending each church function regularly, I would often miss her the most when I was in the church services, especially on youth Sunday because she was a youth leader prior to her departure; so I was always looking at the seat where she would normally sit in church, but there was someone else sitting there instead of Elecia.

On the tenth day after she left home, I went to the morning service at church and planned to visit her home at 8 King Street where the rest of her family was still living. At the time, I continued to fellowship with them because I had always felt like I was a part of the family and was treated in that respect even after Elecia left for America.

After the service ended, I walked up the hill to the home, which was about two miles from the church. Upon approaching their home, I noticed one of Elecia's sisters, Dorett, standing at the door with an unusual bright smile on her face. I knew she was excited to see me, but something told me that she had more than just seeing her sister's ex-fiancé on her mind. As I approached the house, the other family members came rushing toward me with great excitement. I could not understand what was happening in that family at the moment and why the folks were so happy that evening, but I soon found out when I entered the living room of that beautiful Christian home at Titchfield Hill.

When I stepped inside the living room, there was a sudden hush. Elecia's youngest sister, Janet, shouted, "Brother Brown, come right in! I have a surprise for you!" I could not in my wildest dream imagine what this surprise was. However, I walked slowly toward the dining room; I noticed that everyone was seated at the dinner table, ready to eat; so I thought it was a surprise dinner party for me, but for what reason, I could not tell. I noticed all eyes were fixed on a nearby door; then Dorrett asked me to close the door.

As I attempted to close the door, I got the greatest surprise of my life—someone was hiding behind the door, and that someone was Elecia Patterson, the girl of my dreams! My heart leaped with frantic joy when she dashed from behind the door and hugged me tightly; then she began to cry uncontrollably. I was in a state of shock and disbelief, wondering whether I was really seeing Elecia standing in my presence; I thought I was daydreaming in the middle of the afternoon. When I came to myself, there were springs in my steps and butterflies in my stomach. I was speechless for a while, not knowing what to say. But the warm reception she gave me indicated that a new day had just begun in our lives, and indeed, it was. She later told me that she had decided to return to home; she had changed her mind about living abroad. After dinner, she told me the whole truth and the real reason why she came home to the land of her birth. She told us that she was homesick and had been crying for many days because she missed me so much and could not live without me. She confessed that the poem I wrote for her farewell service broke her heart and caused her to reconsider rekindling our relationship.

Our love was rekindled from that very moment; I knew long ago that she was chosen by God to be my decorated bride. I felt as if I was walking on the clouds of heaven when I discovered my love had come back to me again, and this time, it was forever. And even though there were still some lingering thoughts in her mind concerning our future together, she was willing to sacrifice her entire life for me and put all the matrimonial critics of the day to silence. This was a time of great relief for my stressful soul, which was previously under heavy burdens and agony because I was trying to put the broken pieces back together by myself, and there and then, the god of glory stepped right in, calmed my fears, and dried my weeping eyes.

The church folks got the surprise of their lives when she showed up at church next Sunday morning, and the people of the city could not believe their eyes when she appeared in various places in town. Some folks were happy to see her; others were sad and upset when they learned that Elecia had returned to her hometown. Those who were opposed to our relationship were very disturbed to the point where their fury escalated into maximum proportions of anger. Soon, word went out far and wide that she had returned to the city; and like a mad army of ants, some of the church folks went into a frenzy, desiring to put out the love between us and to destroy any possibility of matrimonial plans by any possible means.

Subsequently, my trials multiplied; the burdens of my heart grew heavy as I tried to understand the thought pattern of my countrymen. Prior to this, I was drifting from the shores of haunted memories. Now it was a new beginning of religious persecution that had raised its ugly head against that determined love of ours. This period of our lives marked the beginning of a new era of the testing of my faith in God and my love for Elecia. But I was more determined than ever before to suffer the consequences in order to remain in the will of God for my life and to pursue the road that will ultimately lead to a time of happiness for both of us. I made up my mind that Elecia was going to be my long and lasting love; therefore, I began to set out a course that would ultimately lead to the contemplation of matrimonial agreement. I was contented in my tribulations as a result of my undaunted love for Elecia. She was a fountain of delight and a river of gladness in those moments of my despair. And I held on to her love like a "drowning man reaching for a straw." It seemed like it was the last chance for me to place my signet upon her gentle brow. So I cleaved to that sacred hope without wavering, panting for those golden hours of holy matrimony when she shall say "I do."

In the spring of 1980, wedding bells began to ring in the congregation gathered at 52 West Street. The young people were getting married on a rapid scale. Love was in the air, and the wedding breeze was blowing across the religious arena for several months. Eyes were looking in our direction, positively and negatively. Satan was in the peak of his conference, strategizing his adversaries for an all-out attack on my godly intentions. The consciousness of God's will for my life was foremost on my mind as I sought divine help in this time of decision making. I knew there would have to be an intervention of the Holy Spirit in order for me to survive the onslaught of the enemy of my soul. So I began to commit myself in prayer and weekly fasting with a view to receive strength from God to face what was to come.

My love for Elecia increased significantly after each trial, and some folks could not understand why the bond of love between us was so hard to break. In fact, we ourselves could not fathom the intensity of this love; we seemed to get closer during the times when we were hit hardest by the critics of the day, who thought we were not the right pair for marriage. Persecution began to increase from within and outside the church; some of the church folks questioned everything about our relationship, saying Elecia was not the right person for me, and I was not the right person for her. People seemed to have turned themselves into self-proclaimed deities, trying to determine the course of our lives by personal declarations and ostracism.

There were different groups in the church, each with one view or another why Elecia and I should not be married. Some said we were not compatible; some indicated, "He should marry Sheila." Others preferred Janet.

One woman declared, "He should marry someone who is in the church a long time before Elecia." A few folks remained neutral; some secretly plotted against me with callous intentions to destroy any signs of wedding arrangements. They were steadfast in their quest to extinguish my love for the girl of my dreams and to make my life a public monument of sad remembrance.

This was more than enough for any man in love to encounter and an awful price to pay for choosing a girl to love that was not conducive to their selfish expectations. Elecia's love for me was so strong, it was renting me from the optimistic minds of those who had a serious crush on me and thus ignite their anger to a greater extent where they would stop at nothing in order to achieve their goal, even if it meant insulting to me. My mind began to waver once more as Elecia expressed her thoughts of uncertainty to me concerning our future together, which almost tore my heart apart. I was at a crossroad, depending on God to direct my destiny; and to add to my distress, there arose a great controversy with other young girls who had serious crush on me—some of which I had no knowledge; others I knew about from sources close to me. It was at that point I decided to have a serious talk with Elecia concerning our relationship and the future of our lives.

It was the summer of 1980 on a beautiful August moonlit night when Elecia consented to meet with me to discuss the subject of our relationship and to give me the answer to my final request for marrying her. I wanted to know if she was serious about marrying me or if she was ready to terminate our relationship for good. I was a bit disturbed over the constant uncertainty of her marrying me, so I wanted to hear the truth even if it meant that she would forsake me. That night, I went to 14 Fourteen Folly Road where she was living at that time accompanied by Brother Luther "Tip-Top" Burke. My mind was made up that night that this was going to be the deciding moment of our relationship. I had made up my mind that whichever way it turned out, I would walk away from the scene knowing I had poured out my heart at her feet for the last time.

History recorded that night as the turning point of my life. Elecia and I clearly discussed the many factors of our relationship and the possibility of marriage; on the meeting agenda were the various struggles we encountered over the past three years—insults, persecutions, threats, reproaches, and discouragement from family, friends, and foes—marriage, future plans, and, above all, her decision to marry me or to take her exit from the parkway of my life. I was more determined than ever to hear her final chapter concerning me. I told her, "If I walk through that door tonight without an answer from you concerning marrying me, I will be walking out of your life forever, and God will charge you for breaking my heart." As the meeting continued, the power of the Holy Spirit overshadowed me, and I began to speak in other tongues as the Spirit gave utterance. Elecia was dumbfounded for a while; the fear of God came upon us as the Holy Spirit spoke through me and manifested God's will for our lives to her.

Our called meeting was transformed into a Pentecostal prayer meeting as we wept bitterly before God, asking Him for his direction in our relationship.

I wanted a confirmation from God that night and could not have wanted it more earnestly. God showed up without an invitation and took over the humans' agenda. He spoke audibly to Elecia, Luther, and I through the unexpected vessel of my personhood. I was trembling with fear as the Holy Spirit used me to prophesy to Elecia concerning the will of God for our relationship. I never thought that God would use me to bring closure to the doubts and fears that were surrounding our relationship. We were assured, reaffirmed, and steadfast in our love and commitment to each other. Elecia was absolutely clear in her mind that she wanted to marry me, despite of the odds. She gave me her full assurance and commitment that we were going to be married as soon as possible. I stood my ground and was extremely firm with her in my conviction that God had ordained that we should be together as husband and wife and that she should remove all doubts and fears from her heart. Brother Luther "Tip-Top" Burke was my solemn witness in this supernatural encounter when God showed up at that unconventional meeting and defied all human thoughts. Fear came upon Elecia as I spoke with an unusual boldness on the various factors that were threatening to tear us apart, and she knew then it was impossible to fight with God and win. So she surrendered to His will and made her decision that sacred night of summer to take my hand in holy matrimony.

I left her home that Friday night with a sense of purpose and great aspirations, knowing that she had consented to walk down an aisle somewhere soon and take my hand in marriage without reservation. As I journeyed home, the joy of the Lord was kindled within me, and the hope of a bright future with Elecia was like a golden stream of sweet caress. We knew it was not going to be an easy task breaking the news of a wedding date to the uninvited objectors, but the grace of God that was with me dispelled my fears and calmed my troubled soul. Luther and I walked home slowly. He was convinced that God had spoken that night; he encouraged me along as we journeyed. Nothing could stop me from charting the course toward getting married to Elecia. I had by now fully made up my mind to face whatever may come my way; therefore, I was prepared to face the onslaught of the coming days without wavering

The Lord began to reveal himself to me more clearly as I pondered upon the future. I had a vision that was so clear and seemed so real to me. In that vision, I saw thirty-three young girls, most of them I knew from the church I attended; they were in a circle, having a long conversation. Then I looked across from the park where they were gathered and saw Elecia standing by herself under a tree, and a voice spoke out of the cloud to me, saying, "Those shall turn from you, but the one standing by the tree shall bring you happiness and shall be a fountain of love to you." Her countenance was bright, like that of an angel; there was a shining glow of light, and it overshadowed the place where she was standing. Then suddenly, the other girls stopped their conversation and turned their eyes toward Elecia, standing in the distance; they were conversing, but I could not hear what they were saying. Then they all disappeared from the scene, leaving Elecia standing alone. I approached her and extended my hand toward her; then she suddenly ascended to the sky, leaving me standing with my arm outstretched, and that's when I awoke from the dream.

The vision was clear. It was a confirmation of the first vision I had before. I was convinced in my mind that God had spoken to me; I felt that God has answered my prayer-request for a confirmation concerning our relationship. It was my belief that God came through for me after I have consulted Him for direction on my matrimonial journey. I always wanted something unusual to happen to point me to the will of God, and so it did happen. It was often my practice to request of the Lord to answer my prayers with specific signs so that I will be assured that I was in His perfect will. For me, this was an important factor of the Christian life, living in the perfect will of God; so I cherished this thought with all my heart.

For the rest of that particular year, Elecia and I began serious preparations for our wedding. We kept our plans in secret, conscious of the fact that there were oppositions against us from all angles of life. Our secret plans were classified, but to our shocking surprise, someone leaked the information concerning our wedding plans to the public. It was now noised abroad, and trouble was in the air. During these months of planning, we came under severe persecutions from some of the church folks as well as the unbelievers of the city. After the news broke, I was strictly forbidden from seeing Elecia in public by the order of the church council. I was given a restraining order not to visit Elecia, I was denied visitation rights, and strictly monitored by the elders and mothers of the church if we were seen having a conversation at any church function. If I was seen going into the direction of Elecia's home I would be immediately reported to the elders of the church, and I was forbidden from taking part in church activities when we were allegedly seen in public together.

In those days, it was easier to get to heaven than to become a member of the church of God. One had to pass through the gates of "hell" before he or she could become an approved Christian for heaven. I was caught up into the era of the strictest patriarchs of church history whose motto was "The appearance of evil is evil." Those who walked the path of Christendom had to pass the test of time in order to secure a rightful place in the Christian Hall of Fame and in the kingdom of eternity. The struggles continued with full force, with an objective far from anything godly. It was the personal pursuits of others, with a view to satisfy the ego of one preference over another. My personal life became a public show. I was the speech of men's tongues and the subject of most family's dining table discussions; my private life was the main motion on the agendas of much church council meeting. Our relationship was the talk of the town, the center of attraction, the hybrid of sorrow, the companion of burdens, and the intense moment of expectancy to many young Christian girls who desired my hand in marriage. However, to Elecia, I was the shining armor of the early church, a prophet, sent from God with a burning in his bosom and the love of a lifetime, which came upon her golden hills and stole her heart away. On the other hand, there were those who could not be contented with such romantic audacity, without a fight to disrupt a union so nobly planned.

In theory, I was brought to the courtroom of popular demands by the unauthorized judges of the day, and my only crime was *falling in love* with a woman so comely, created in sweet delight; she was a light in my dark room and the sunshine on my cloudy days, one who loved life and lived it with love. Her captivating smiles could warm a cold heart of sadness, and her soul reached out to the lonely and sad. If love was a crime that was punishable by death, I would have died for a most worthy cause at the hands of my oppressors. The savage attacks on my character could not detour the vehicle that transported my beaming heart of love to Elecia Patterson, the girl of my dreams.

Our main methods of communication were mostly by telephone and secret love letters, delivered privately and confidentially by Sister Joan "Skinny" Scott, who acted as our unofficial postal delivery person during that period of our courtship. We had to distance ourselves from each other in order to avoid confrontation with some church folks. We knew that we were deeply in love with each other, but many people felt otherwise. Some even went as far as to tell me whom I should marry; others felt Elecia was the wrong girl for me, and some thought I was the wrong guy for her. Our love story became a public fiesta and a sad parade of masquerading objectors, canvassing for the extinction of such indelible love that was founded upon divine principles and approval that baffled the minds of discontented humanity.

As a result of my seemingly impertinent confession of love for Elecia to the authority of the church, I came under fire; I was dubbed barefaced and too bold for my age, out of order, naïve, too young to get marry, innocent, and inexperienced. I defied all these notions by expressing my love for Elecia more openly and without fear; this stirred up more anger among the critics of the day, who intensified their quest to disrupt any sign of wedding plans. The struggles continued one after the other for several more months; there seemed to be no end in sight and no sign of peaceful coexistence among our family and friends who were too consumed with their ideologies and concepts of a perfect match for their son and daughter who were embarking upon a new horizon that was conflicting to the views of most well-intentioned person of that religious era.

The days ahead had problems printed on every side of our lives as we strived toward setting a wedding date and to make known our hearts' desire to our pastor, the Reverend F. A. Beason, before publishing the wedding bond. We attended several counseling sessions with our pastor in preparation for marriage. Our pastor was very stern, prompt, and aggressive in his deliberations. His eyes were always red as blood; when I looked at him, it seemed like fire was in his eyes, especially when he preached. I feared the God in him so much that I was afraid of staying in his presence for an extended period of time. Rev. Beason was my mentor, my father, my confidant, and my priest who took my request to the Lord. He was the pastor who pushed us toward excellence. He was responsible for our spiritual growth and maturity in the Christian faith, a great man of God whom the Lord used mightily in those days to do miracles and wonders in the congregation of the righteous. As a result of Rev. Beason's sound biblical teachings and advice, Elecia and I survived the tests and persecutions of that period. Therefore, words are inadequate to express our gratefulness to this noble man of God for molding our lives every step of the way. He was responsible for our success on life's journey and will be remembered from now and always till the days dawn and the shadows flee from my sacred eyes.

After much thought and planning, Elecia and I decided to get married on Saturday, May 2, 1981, at 4:00 p.m. in our home church at 52 West Street. We discussed this with our pastor, and he agreed to perform the wedding ceremony. As we were making plans to print the invitations, the news of our upcoming wedding began to spread all over town and across the seas to foreign lands. Some of the church folks were perturbed, upset, and outraged as a result of this breaking news; various groups in the congregation assembled privately to discuss the issue of our pending marriage. There were numerous schools of thought emerging rapidly who posited their matrimonial theories on the inquisitive minds of the common man. The known objectors of the marriage became high rated while the secret ones were revealed to foster public participation in the quest to disrupt our wedding.

By the beginning of the New Year 1981, those opposed to our wedding were upbeat, vigilant, and determined to launch a public protest. They were not afraid to state their objections to the pastor, church leaders, my parents, and other relatives. Some tried to influence members of own my family to rebel against the marriage and to boycott the wedding. There were reports that a public demonstration was organized for the wedding day where a group of church folks would march through the town dressed in black to make known their disapproval of the marriage between Elecia and me. This was a very sad moment in time for us. We were now looking forward to a time of tranquility, but instead, we received disappointing news of deep despair. To add to this nerve-racking saga, there were reports that some of the alleged perpetrators involved in this plan were members of the church.

It was scarring, thought-provoking, and discouraging for Elecia and me as we sought for a better way to put an end to this utter madness. We were faced with a dilemma, not knowing what course of action to take from there forward after we learned of this new development at such a crucial time. Elecia was fearful, but determined to go forward with our wedding plans, despite the distractions of the objectors. We sought the help of God and our pastor to guide us out of this turbulence. Our pastor counseled with us, prayed with us, and gave his best advice in such a difficult situation. He instructed us to change our wedding date in order to avoid predestined confrontations and recommended to us some marriage officers in the capital city of Kingston, whom we could contact regarding performing the wedding ceremony. This was a heartrending decision making for us as our only desire was for our own pastor to do the honors on our special day. Our dream was completely shattered; however, we were aware of the fact that this was the best course of action to embark upon at the time. We have waited for three and a half years, and now the time had come for this climax of a golden milestone, but the enemy of our souls refused to quit without a fight, so a great expectation was now turned into a great disappointment. It was one of the great sadness of my heart that came upon my finite being on the twilight of a grand tomorrow when I learned that our pastor, the Reverend F. A. Beason, will not be able to join us together in holy matrimony. Therefore, we had no other alternative but to resort to another plan of action.

After serious consideration, we decided to choose the Reverend Ronald A. Blair, the then pastor of the Eastwood Park New Testament Church of God, to be our marriage officer. So we contacted him shortly afterward and made the necessary preparation for the journey to the big city. At this point, we realized that we had to go on the defensive in order to keep this new plan top secret, or else we would be up for a rude awakening. The wedding invitations were sent out to the invited guests dated May 2, 1981. Elecia and I decided on a new date—April 18, 1981, at 9:00 a.m. The original date was still standing, and the guests were making their final preparations for the wedding day. We decided that nothing was going to hinder us from getting married, except death or the second coming of Christ. So we planned to elope to Kingston, the capital city, in order to get married. Only a few persons had any knowledge of the new plans, including our parents, family members, and my close friend Trucky. These persons were given strict instruction not to leak the plan to anyone. We treated this as classified, confidential information.

The plans of the enemy were still intact, breathing out threats against us openly from all angles of the society. Despite of those threats to disrupt the wedding plans, God was on the job, securing a safe passage for us across the swelling tides of life's restless sea. According to reports, the planned protest was still on the agenda for May 2; members of that posse were busy getting their black outfits, ready for the "kill." However, while men on earth were planning to do evil, God in heaven was wiping out their plans and charting a new course for Elecia and me. The atmosphere became very tense as it drew nearer toward the end of March. For most people, it was a month and a few days remaining before the wedding bells began to sound; but for those who knew otherwise, it was only nineteen days that separated us from the bosom of each other as we yearned for that bright tomorrow.

Elecia's amazing love surpassed the boundaries of the coming adversities and gave me an insight into that glad future. I knew then that nothing good comes easy, and the burdens I bore in my sojourn have brought hope and faith to guide me along the way. As I recapitulate, I recognized that the days of my life almost ended up in the general hospital as a result of the young and the restless objectors of my intimate love for the girl I most adored. As the world turns, I thought of another world where there will be neither pain nor sorrow to haunt this soul of mine in that blessed land of light far beyond the cloudy skies of that great and golden morrow.

While pondering on the coming day of gladness, my heart longed for Elecia's love to cover me with sweet embrace. She was indeed a woman nobly created with captivating delight, built by the architect of the universe, and thus predestined for the bosom of a county boy like me. I loved her more than cooked food and cherished the joy she brought into my life forevermore. Her love for me was without question unconditional and true; she had a touch of class and a sense of magnanimity, which transcended to my being and caused me to pause at the chime of her voice and the smell of her presence. I was doing my very best to keep my composure while I waited for the wedding day, but anxiety was getting the upper hand of me. The more I thought of her, the more I longed for her to come close to my bosom that I may embrace her once and then forever. My love for her was boiling up inside like a rolling tide upon the restless sea. I waited and waited, with a panting heart, for the day to come when our hearts would beat as one.

Others were trying to demolish the unbroken bond that bound us together, but no force from any side of the fence of hell could extinguish the fire of love that burned within us for each other, nor could any obstacles—small or great—detour our steps from that coveted altar where millions before said "I do." We kept our hopes bright and our faith in God strong; notwithstanding, we could not ignore the thoughts that haunted us as a result of the planned disturbances. Due to the hostile climate at the time, anything was possible, so we did not want to take the slightest chance in ignoring the angry folks that would probably ruin our sacred wedding day. We were playing it safe, keeping a cool head in the heat of the remaining days before the wedding. We had already chosen our best man and maid of honor, and they knew that that day was to remain a secret until the matrimonial tale was told. We wanted to avoid any signs of trouble that were brewing

Fallen in love

in the hearts of some disgruntled members of the congregation and so we kept the date secretly in order not to give those opposed to the marriage any hint of our new wedding plans.

This was indeed one of the most unforgettable times of my life as I had to make some of the most serious and far-reaching decisions that, of course, would determine my destiny. Therefore, I must thank the Almighty God who had lavished me with His mercies and grace and caused my soul to rejoice in the god of my salvation. I was extremely grateful to the Lord Jesus Christ, my personal savior and friend, who had enabled me to overcome my fears, frustrations, and burdens on this rigged and twisted part of my Christian journey. I was more convinced that the course ahead was filled with hope and cheer as I approached the day of holy matrimony. Despite of the burdens I carried as a result of falling in love with Elecia, I never lost focus on the girl I loved, the one and only angel of light that came my way and I knew that we were meant for each other and both for the Lord.

My eyes were now set on that new horizon, on that special scene where our hearts would unite as one and grow fonder from that day forward. I had many sleepless nights during those last days of March to early April, knowing that I was embarking upon a very serious avenue of life that would change the course of history for me, personally, for Elecia and ultimately for the congregation of which I was an integral part for many years. I was conscious of my divine calling, which I had to safeguard, and the sacred trust that was invested in me by God and my fellow men. Therefore, I continued to uphold the Christian faith lay down by my predecessors as I sought God from deep within my heart for His guidance in the remaining days prior to the wedding date.

I prayed and fasted for strength from God, not only to prepare us for the possible demonstration on the wedding day, but also to face some of my family members, relatives, and church folks later after the announcement is made in the church that we were married. Prior to our departure to the capital city, our pastor advised us to return to church the next day after the wedding so that he could formally introduce us to the congregation as husband and wife. This we finally agreed to and pledged in our hearts to honor the plan. Elecia and I had no clue what was going to be the reactions of the saints gathered at 52 West Street when this unexpected announcement was made. However, our minds were made up to face any adversities of the future together.

It was on the eve of the big day. I sat up most of the night. A sea of thoughts flashed across my mind. Everything was finalized earlier that day concerning our travel plans to the capital city, Kingston. There was some amount of fear in me, mingled with excitement that captured the most part of that memorable night. I thought about the past trials and tribulations, the journey to the city, my parents, siblings, relatives, friends, and enemies who have not known that I was about to be married a few short hours away. I knew there was going to be serious consequences from all sources, but I also knew that I was not going to face them by myself, but with my beloved wife and the good Lord up above. During the long, long night, I talked to God and placed all my care in His hands, praying for journeying mercies and comfort for all who was to take the historic trip on that unknown tomorrow.

The morning of April 18 was closing in on me faster than I could think. My soul leaped with joy and praise like a cloudburst from the eastern sky. My spirit began to rejoice with immense joy as I reminisced on the long, long journey of my childhood days to where I was that night. Cognizant of the fact that the trip was very early in the morning, I tried to sleep but could not wink my eyes at all or slumber, but only pondered over every step of the next day and what the future would hold for Elecia and me. Our mission was clear; our minds were affixed on 39 Chestervale Avenue, Kingston, Jamaica. We planned on taking public transportation to the capital city, eloping from all possible obstacles that threatened the well-being of our quest to fulfill the will of God for our lives.

The anonymous objectors of those relentless days of struggles were unaware of the fact that we were ahead of the game because while they were plotting to disrupt the original wedding day, we were finalizing plans to elope to another part of the country and get married on a new appointed date. They had a mission; we had our too, but only that theirs were known and ours unknown—a secret so tightly kept from all and sundry, friends and foes. For many years, it seemed impossible, but now it became a bright promise and a dream coming true for Elecia and me.

History was about to be recorded soon, about sixty-five miles away. Elecia and I were destined to write the first chapter of an intriguing memoir. We were on a very serious avenue of fundamental truth where God was guiding, and we were following His instructions on the road to holy matrimony.

No doubt, I was eager to get to that destination and subsequently kissed away the pain from her heart when I arrived at the place appointed, then exchanged our vows without fears, and laid her down on a bed of roses on that romantic night of sweet repose, where only love and peace abode.

That sacred hour was fast approaching, that time when the hidden mystery was to be revealed in a city of unhidden secrets where news spread faster than wildfire. The hours that followed brought much to my memory as I pondered on the things that provoked my thoughts during the past night. The girl of my dreams occupied the center of my thoughts for the remaining hours of the night, wondering if she was all right. We had no telephone connection, and to add to that, we were living about ten miles apart. Therefore, it was somewhat painstaking for me. However, I knew in my heart that she was thinking about me and praying for my strength in the Lord while I was doing the same for her.

By this time, many of the church folks thought the wedding was either postponed or cancelled due to the fact that many persons were totally against us getting married. Some people just didn't have a clue what to expect from this long and lasting relationship between Elecia and me. There were ongoing discussions, private meetings, plots, disagreements, criticisms, and misguided indulgence in progress even as the early dawn drew near. Some of the trusted saints of Christendom got caught up in the secret web of deception as a result of the blatant misunderstanding of a few good citizens of God's kingdom. This escalated into complete religious mayhem at the expense of two persons that were madly in love. On the other hand, there were others who prayed earnestly for us that God's will be done in our lives. Had it not been for the grace of God upon my life and the prayers of some old veterans of the faith, my end would be bitter, and my tale would be tragic. So I gave thanks to the great God of heaven, who saw the coming storms and delivered me from the body of my afflictions.

God opened my spiritual eyes; I could see angels protecting me in my days of darkness and unquenched burdens as I journeyed toward the New Jerusalem. Amid the silent lonely days, I was sustained by the faith and courage of knowing Christ in a real personal way. The sacred songs and scriptures rapture my soul into godly ecstasy, causing sadness and crying to be transformed into singing and serenity. My eyes were fixed on god and my heart rejoiced, knowing that if God permitted, the hour would come when we would get married and have a grand ball on our wedding day. Now the final moment was fast approaching, and everything was ready as planned; it was going to be a very small privately held wedding in the capital city of our homeland. This day was about to close one chapter of my life and open another; and though unknown to me, I ventured upon it without fear, like a man taking a blind leap into the dark, not knowing where his feet would land. Nevertheless, I proceeded with love and laughter, hoping to present my finite life to my comely bride on a platter of romance and then to wish for her a fountain of love and rivers of happiness.

CHAPTER SEVEN
THE EFFECTS OF THE STRUGGLES

In the midst of the struggle, my mind worked more vigorously than ever before and probably filled my days with wishful thinking. When the Saturday morning came, the ground was covered with frost and dew from the overnight raindrops, and the sun peeped through the dark clouds across the eastern skies. I knew then that this was the day of a new horizon in my life. It was April 18, 1981, when we boarded the minibus bound for the capital city of Kingston. I got dressed very early that Saturday morning, crept quietly out of the house, and walked about five miles to the bus stop where I waited for Elecia, Dorrett, and Lloyd (Toney) to arrive on the bus that was coming from the town of Port Antonio destined for Kingston. I prayed that no one from the church would see me on the street that ungodly hour of the morning, or else I would be thoroughly questioned concerning my early-morning expedition.

It was about six a.m. when the bus arrived at the Bound Brook Square. I recognized the driver, and then I knew it was the right bus that we had planned to travel on. Sure enough, the others were on board, so I greeted them with joy as the bus sped away from the village of Bound Brook. Presumably, by this time, the folks in town were fast asleep while we slipped out of sight before daybreaks and the shadows fled away. With the realization of any expectations from the opposing folks, I was conscious of the serious decision making. Therefore, with typical faith, prayers and promise, I managed to overcome some of the posttraumatic difficulties of our courtship by embarking upon changing the entire feature of my life, consoled by the tone and balance of God's answer to prayed prayers of the past.

As we journeyed, many thoughts and various flashbacks of past conflicts and tests from some of the church folks came to me. I could not have held back the tears from my eyes as I sat in the minibus. I was tensed, frightened, happy, and sad at the same time, yet conscious of God's will for my life because I knew this was the journey that was going to change the status of my life. In those two and a half hours of traveling, Dorrett and Toney encouraged us and gave full moral support all the way to Kingston. They were towers of strength to us, standing in the gap with 100 percent support. This helped lift our spirits as we drew near to the location where the wedding was to take place.

We arrived at the minister's house in 39 Chestervale Avenue at 8:30a.m, half an hour before the scheduled wedding ceremony. The minister, Rev. Ronald A. Blair, welcomed us warmly and sat us down in his living room while his hospitable wife, Evon, entertained us with refreshments. After a short time, Rev. Blair returned to the living room well dressed in his clergy attire. My brother-in-law Lloyd was the best man; he and I were dressed in suits, but not the usual wedding suits we would normally wear on a typical wedding day. Elecia and her sister Dorrett was beautifully arrayed, but unfortunately, not in bridal gowns because the original date for the wedding was May 2; and we planned to have the wedding reception where we would wear our wedding apparel.

The ceremony began precisely at nine o'clock. While we stood before the minister, the tears kept running down my eyes; then suddenly, everyone in the wedding party began crying while Rev. Blair was conducting the ceremony. We made our vows to each other in tears, mingled with joy and happiness. The small gathering of six was very emotional as the minister made the final pronunciation upon us and prayed a moving prayer of dedication. Our dress code was elegantly casual. We had no camera, photographer, or videographer; and there was no one or nothing to capture the splendor and glory of that sacred moment. We were just ordinary folks with extraordinary ambitions, to have and to hold each other from that day forward. Rev. Blair and his wife congratulated us and gave us his blessing. Elecia and I hugged each other tightly, and we both burst into uncontrollable tears, which moved the small wedding party to tears. It was a moment that no one present could truly explain; the Holy Spirit was evident in that house and ministered to our hearts that morning in no uncertain manner. Our wedding apparel were still at the designer's store being prepared for the original date, May 2; this was one of the factors that broke our hearts, knowing that we had to precede our wedding date eloping to the capital city in order to avoid the objectors. However, we thanked God for having allowed us to cross the boisterous sea of our lives.

Rev. Blair charged us with a compelling word from the scriptures; and at that precious moment, we knew that the chains of sadness were broken, sorrow and sighing were over, and a new day was dawning. The anointed man of God spoke as he was directed by the Holy Spirit. He had the gift of discernment of Spirit; it seemed as if he knew everything about us. He obviously discerned the things we had gone through during the three years of courtship. It was our first time meeting Rev. Blair, yet it seemed that he knew everything about us. The burdens fell from my back as he pronounced us husband and wife; I was released from a heavy load as we walked out of the man of God house with a deep settled peace in our souls. We bid farewell to the family and left with unquenched joy and complete wonderment. We began a new life that day—two hearts beating as one, founded on the premise of absolute captivating love. We held on to each other tightly as we walked away from that blessed home where history had just been made.

The great expectation was realized on that cloudless morning of spring when we entered upon a new beginning. The dark night had passed, and the day broke with glorious sunshine of sweet romance upon my tinted brow. Alas! I sang with melody in my soul and walked out of that sacred place with springs in my steps and magnanimity in my breast as the memories of the dark past slowly bid farewell from my frantic bosom to that uninhabited land beyond the maze. I had conquered my fears, braved the rolling tides of the enemy, and silenced the voices of the critics. Now my love was full and the way before me clear; the rain had stopped falling on the corner of my untimely procrastinations, and I was now ready to take on the world without hesitation. So I went on my way—singing, shouting, dancing, and praising the god of our fathers without reservation.

The return trip was filled with excitement, which compensated for the horror of the past and the burdens on my journey from courtship to the matrimonial altar. I must confess that that day was one of the best days of the rest of my life. I contended to place my soul on an avenue of praises and gratitude toward God my creator. We made several stops on the way home, resulting in us getting home in the twilight hour, which turned out perfect for us, not wanting anyone to see us together before the official announcement was made at church. The people in my town had no knowledge that we were married; otherwise, there would have been some amount of disturbance. That blessed evening of sweet romance was over, I wondered, how we were going to slip back quietly into the town unnoticed.

Upon reaching the city, we requested of the bus driver to take us straight to our new home at 14 Folly Road, a few miles on the outskirts of the town near the seacoast. This was our first matrimonial home, and upon reaching home, we knelt down at the bedside and prayed, giving thanks to the good Lord up above for His goodness toward us. We then called our pastor, Rev. F. A. Beason, on the phone to let him know we were back in town. He congratulated us and wished us God's blessing; he encouraged us to attend church the next day. This, of course, was very unusual; but we took his advice, which was a sound one. The fact that most of the church folks were unaware that we were married; it was the best thing to do to clear all doubts that might arise as a result of us being together. We then discussed the matter at dinner and then prepared ourselves for church next day. This was the first night of the rest of our lives together.

Sunday morning came; I was up early, filled with anxiety and some amount of suppressed fears. After family devotion we had our first breakfast together as a husband and wife. After this we began our journey to the house of God at 52 West Street. Normally, I stood at one of the doors of the church because I was serving as an usher. However, I went into the church and sat down with Elecia, leaving many onlookers speculating. This was our first time sitting together in church for more than three years. Therefore, this was really an unusual situation for me. Our wedding bands glittered on our fingers, but still, no one took any notice. However, the service was in high gear as usual; and I was getting even more nervous, knowing that, that moment of public declaration concerning our recent wedding was about to be made by our pastor, Rev. F. A. Beason, to the congregation.

I was not quite sure what to expect that morning, but I knew it wasn't going to be a smooth day in God's house when this shocking revelation came to light. So I braced myself for the unexpected, with a word of prayer to the good man upstairs who had heard me in the past when I called upon Him. After all the announcements were made, our pastor welcomed another couple, Mr. and Mrs. Gary Welsh, who had just returned from their honeymoon on the north coast of the island; and the church stood up and gave a thunderous applause. The pastor then paused for a few minutes and said, "We have in our midst this morning a newlywed couple. They were married just yesterday." The entire congregation went silent; folks were looking around to see which couple was about to stand. The pastor then asked, "Will Mr. and Mrs. Aubrey C. H. Brown stand please." Suddenly, there was a hush, a perfect silence in the church for a few minutes. Then there were outbursts of various exclamations and expressions; in fact, most of the church folks were upset for one reason or another.

Those who were opposed to us getting married were utterly astonished; they were left in shock and utter disbelief. Some were annoyed while others were speechless, left with a sudden impact and total wonderment. Others who had a crush on me had their dreams shattered—some cried; others fainted. Most of the people stood still—forlorn, disappointed, and brokenhearted. A few of the older folks rejoiced. The excited morning's worship was transformed into a confused disrupted audience of countless frantic fractions. It was certainly not an easy task for the man of God, though heavily anointed, to reach some Christian folks on that unforgettable Sunday morning of spring when he preached the Word of God from the sacred podium. The congregation was tense; you could see some of people's body language clearly. The brethren took their eyes off the sacred podium and focused their attention on Elecia and me—some with love, others with vengeance and wrath. A few "amen," "praise the Lord," and "hallelujah" was uttered by the blood-washed saints of Zion; this gave us assurance that there were a few in the church that were still on our side of the fence.

After the service ended, it was time to face the fury of the folks. I was personally assaulted, verbally and physically, by some of the brethren who confronted me without fear. Some pointed their fingers in my face, some pulled my coat, and others dragged me by my arms. A few sisters cut their eyes at me; some passed by, stared at me, and walked away in anger. I was called "wicked," "deceiver," "Judas," and "traitor" to name a few by some of the sisters in particular who were opposed to me marrying Elecia. My oldest sister, Miretta, slapped me in my head from behind, then hugged me, and began to cry profusely; she was upset because she wanted to be at my wedding. She was totally disappointed in me for eloping to get married. The beautiful day of worship was transformed into an ecclesiastical disturbance. The saints expressed themselves to Elecia and me without reservation. They wouldn't hold anything back; they let us have it all, and when they finished speaking, we did not know if we could stand.

Folks from all over surrounded me in front of the church building that afternoon, asking various questions concerning our decision to get married earlier than the planned date. I was brought before the grand jury of public opinion where I received the lashes of the tongues of my objectors. I could not escape the confused, troubled, and boisterous crowd that held me captive on the pavement of the Battle Factory Church at 52 West Street. Nor was there any mercy from my persistent executioners, who were ready to slay me in the open public. I was standing, trembling, before my judges and juries, waiting to be sentenced to a state of religious excommunication from my own denomination.

Among those who were most disappointed were the ones who were planning to demonstrate against the wedding on the day in question. Their plans were shattered when they learned that our wedding preceded the proposed date. Some of the older Christians were very happy for us and congratulated us for the bold steps that we had taken in getting married. I recalled that Sunday morning as the crowd gathered around me in much disgust, wanting to take matters into their own hand; but there came Sister Ida Wallace, a veteran in the faith. She broke through the massive crowd, came to where I was standing, shook my hand, looked me in my eyes, and said, "So you are a conqueror, Brother Brown." Then she quickly walked away and disappeared from the scene. These words could not be erased from my mind, and even now, they still linger in my thoughts. Sister Wallace later went home to be with the Lord and left me with the solemn belief that I could be a conqueror over all my circumstances. These words resonated with me from that day forward as I tried to overcome the plans of the enemy against my soul. There were others who gave us great support and encouragement during that troubled period of my life.

Chief among those were our pastor, Rev. F. A. Beason, mother Linda Scott, Mother McKenzie, Mother Mary Curtis, Brother Easton "Peanut" Thompson, Brother Michael Coulson, Brother Edwin Maxwell, Sister Joan 'skinny' Scott and Brother Luther "Tip-Top" Burke, Brother Balford 'trucky' Curtis, Brother and sister Gary Welsh, who got married a few days before us, among others. These precious saints of God were a tower of strength to me on that sad day of the great matrimonial disclosure.

Soon, our wedding story became the talk of the town; we were encouraged not to worry because the criticisms will only be a nine-day talk.

Listening to this popular phrase of the day seemed good, but the experience of that Sunday morning conflict contradicted my finite mind, and I was left to contend that it would be an awful long time before things would return to normality. In fact, this was the preface of the writings of a new era of struggles, which was to last for many months and perhaps years. Most of my close friends became my foes due to the fact that Elecia and I got married. There were some church folks who refused to have fellowship with me. I became an outcast, a stranger, among my brethren and an alien in my own church and community, despised and rejected by some relatives and close friends because of the choice I made to marry the *girl of my dreams*. If it was possible, some folks would have blotted my name out of the lamb's Book of Life and prevented me from entering the portals of heaven when the pearly gates are opened In all of this, God was my helper; through these trials and tribulations, the Lord kept me focused on the prize ahead.

We were now settled in our new life, living as husband and wife, but there were others who were still bitter and would not associate themselves with us. Perhaps if God had sent Jesus to take the church home, many would have been left behind in that cold winter of their Christian walk. We were constantly criticized, cold-shouldered, and buffeted by some of our own church folks who refused to accept the fact that we were married. Some even refused to call or write Elecia's name not wanting to recognize her as Mrs. Brown. Our marriage was always under the scrutiny of the public and the church from the first day onward, and we were quite aware of that; so we lived our lives as an open book before our fellowmen, manifesting the unchanging love that bound our hearts together as one. There was a deep settled peace within me, living in the sunshine of life with my wife, Elecia, close by my side every step of the way. Waiting for the original wedding date to come so we could have the chance to wear our wedding apparel and show the world for real that we have crossed that sacred part, when we shall parade down the city's streets in a limousine, then we would have a ball and invite our friends to share in the grand celebration.

On May 2, 1981 the original wedding day, Elecia and I decided to have the wedding reception and to wear our wedding garments as planned. We invited family, relatives, and friends to share this special day with us at our home in 14 Folly Road, Port Antonio. After a citywide drive out, we returned home to join those waiting at the reception. Upon our arrival, they began playing the song "Bless Them Lord, bless them Lord, on Their Wedding Day." Elecia stole the entire show when she alighted from the

The effects of the struggles—I thee wed

The effects of the struggles—for better or worse

decorated car in her elegant, breathtaking bridal gown. The photographers were scrambling all over the place in order not to miss one pose of the photogenic bride. As her graceful feet touched the salubrious lawn of our home, the evening of celebration began. The dashing bride approached the jubilant guests seated with a captivating smile that warmed the hearts of her guests with radiant glows. The aroma of her sweet fragrance penetrated the atmosphere with irresistible captivation. She was a beauty to behold and a gem of delight to look upon she was nobly constructed and magnificently built—a source of sweet caress, a pearl of priceless value, and a rose picked from the garden of sweet romance, a girl with a heart of gold and incomparable sensuality.

It was an evening of splendor and calm serenity as we dined in fine style in an atmosphere of fun, food, and fellowship with loved ones. We received numerous wedding gifts from the guests, as well as words of encouragement and advice from our pastor, Rev. F. A. Beason, who also gave the blessing. That grand evening of unquenched joy and shared pleasure remained in our hearts forever. We sat at ease with those who came to lavish us with unconditional love after such a horrendous time of constant misconceptions and persistent persecutions. The fact that we have crossed that milestone was enough to celebrate the realization of a long-awaited dream, and thereto, we pledged our hearts to each other and to serve the living God with humble pride.

Many of the people in the city thought we were just getting married on that day, not realizing that we were already married on April 18. So the city folks looked and watched with wonder as the 1960 model fish-tail Chevrolet motorcar drove past their residence, carrying Elecia and me to the place where the reception was held.

In the end, it turned out to be a glorious day of celebration, one that resonated in the minds of some of the folks who came to wish us Godspeed on this new journey of life.

We cherished the memories of that day and pledged to keep it alive throughout our marriage. This blessed day continued to serve as a citadel of strength and determination in the onward march of our lives as we enrolled in the matrimonial university as students of the unfeigned love that would not let us go. From there on, we decided to live our lives in love, each for the other, so that others would emulate us as we live out the true meaning of happiness in marriage.

The reception was followed by a trip to London, England, on our honeymoon departing on May 7, 1981. We departed the country from the Norman Manley International Airport on a British Airways flight to the Heathrow International Airport in London. This was my first trip out of the country; I was very excited and anxious to travel abroad. We stopped in Nassau, Bahamas, and Bermuda before arriving in London early the next morning. It was a glorious flight filled with excitement and romance; we had our own private bedroom on the plane and were treated royally by the flight attendants, who pampered us all the way to London. The duration of the flight was close to fourteen hours, but we never got tired or felt restless at any time because the hospitable crew took extra care of us in the first-class cabin.

When we arrived in London, it was very cold and foggy outside, but the warm welcome that we received from Uncle Aston and Aunt Maye took away all our fears of the British weather. They drove us from the airport to their beautiful home at Gosberton Road, Balham, in southwest London, where we spent our honeymoon. We were very grateful for that golden opportunity to have gone to England for the first time in our lives. When we reached Balham, it was half past ten in the morning; and being jet-lagged, we soon fell asleep after having a sumptuous breakfast prepared by Aunt Maye for us. We slept for a very long time, and when we awoke, it felt like a few days had gone by; and because the time zone was different from our homeland, we were totally confused to the point where we thought it was morning when in fact, it was almost five o'clock in the afternoon. Uncle Aston and Aunt Maye had a hard time trying to convince us that it was afternoon and not morning as we supposed.

Now it was dinnertime. Aunt Maye pulled out her touch of fine British cuisine with her Caribbean spirit inherited from Daniel's River. The entire family gathered to eat in a mode of family reunion. They gave us the heartiest welcome in their beautiful home at Gosberton Road. That classic moment was one of the high points of our visit to our motherland. It was the first time that I was meeting Elecia's folks, and there and then, I felt they were my own flesh and blood. They treated me as a prince; I was pampered, lavished with love, and kindly spoken off by everyone whom I met for the first time. Soon, I became an integral part of Uncle Aston and Aunt Maye's family without any reservation.

We had only one problem and that of trying to get adjusted to the different time; and as a result of that, most of our time for the first few days was spent in bed—not necessarily because we were on our honeymoon, but we had a hard time figuring out what time of day it was. Uncle Aston began to tease us, saying, "It seems like you guys only want to stay upstairs and make babies. How can you come to London and not visit Buckingham Palace? That's Cats altogether." He was the funniest person I have ever met; he could give jokes early morning or late at night and get you cracking up all over. He had a tremendous appetite for life and enjoyed every moment of it at any cost.

I once told him that the man was the head of the house; he started laughing hysterically and said, "Not in England. The woman is the head of the house here, look! Margaret Thatcher is the prime minister. If you tell my wife that, she will put me out!" Uncle Aston never ceased to amuse me all the days of our stay in their home.

After a few days, he finally got us out of the house, and we began our tour of the historic sites of England. We toured various interesting spots, including Buckingham Palace, Big Ben, the Greenwich Time (where the world's time clock is set), Piccadilly Circus, and Bull Ring, the world biggest shopping mall, to name a few. Every day was filled with new excitement with Uncle Aston, Aunt Maye, their daughter, Jackie, and grandsons Emmanuel and Joel who taught us the whole culture of England. There was not a sad day with Uncle Aston as he was the chief entertainer in the house; he had a bundle of energy and laughter that would cheer the heart of a dying man back to life. There was never a dull moment with him; his humor kept us going all day long. Shopping with Jackie was full of fun; it was a great experience. She took us all over the city of London on a daily shopping spree. We went to Balham High Road, Tooting, Decford, Trafalgar Square, shepherd Bush, Claphan Common, Brixton, and other shopping places on a regular basis.

I had one of the greatest dreams of my life come true when Uncle Aston took me to Lords the world-famous cricket ground; for many years, I watched the game on television and never thought the day would come when I would set foot on that hollow ground of fame. Thanks to my uncle for making this happen; it was a chance of a lifetime, and I could not resist the offer.

My good friend David McFarlane, a police officer stationed in the London metropolitan area, was there with us on what we called the Men Trip. David was born in England, but he came to live in Jamaica at a tender age; there we met and became close like real brothers, growing up together in the Battle Factory Church. This was a grand reunion for us, not seeing each other for many years. When we arrived in London, we searched all over for David and eventually found out he was assigned to the Brixton Police Station. During those days, there were serious racial riots at Brixton; therefore, he had to work undercover because of the violence as there were very few black police officers in the force at the time, which added more fury to the racial problems of the day. After we I finally found him, the reunion and fun seemed endless; and from that moment, we began to travel all over the country, from Croydon to Balham, from Manchester to Birmingham. We were on the road night and day with Uncle Aston.

We were engaged in a number of old-time cooking, eating fish and chips late at night while watching movies, telling stories of the past, and catching up where we left off for the past ten years. Jackie was always there with us while the boys went to the Gathering. Aunt Maye went to sleep; and Uncle Aston would go to his favorite pub, the Duke, up Balham Road to have a drink and play dominoes with his blokes. I will always remember Uncle Aston's favorite phrase, "It's Cats altogether, isn't it?" The folks in London were a gem of delight to be around; there was never a dull moment in the house or when going anywhere with them.

The day finally came when we had to leave London, the place that we called our home for two weeks. It was a sad farewell at the airport as we cried, hugged, and kissed our relatives goodbye. I could not erase the memories of the past two weeks from my mind as we bid farewell to the British folks who had become my closest kinfolks for a lifetime. Now we had to depart the coveted motherland of disciplinarians to that of our own once more. This was an experience that we cherished since we first set foot on the beautiful shores of England. It was bittersweet for me to say goodbye to them because those past weeks have left a mark of sweet reunion upon me that I would not exchange for anything in this world. We boarded our flight destined for home; the plane taxied down the runway and departed to the sky, leaving them standing in the far distance. My heart broke; I was moved to tears as I reflected on the past two glorious weeks spent at Gosberton Road.

The long, but enjoyable flight ended as the captain landed the aircraft safely on the runway at the Norman Manley International Airport to the thunderous applause of the grateful passengers. We were home at last, excited to see the glorious sunshine in the place we called home—Jamaica, the land we loved. We gave thanks to the Lord for having brought us home safe and for having kept us over these passing days while we were away in England. We then boarded the ground transportation to Port Antonio in the late hours of the night; we traveled around the east coast of the island. I slept most of the way, being tired and jet-lagged from the flight, arriving home close to dawn.

After this, we began to set some serious goals for the future, including purchasing our own home, furthering our education, and having children. Our lives started to blossom in the prosperity of God's grace as the light of Christ shone upon our pathway each day. We had a close bond of togetherness, love, mutual respect, care, and understanding for each other. We then settled down in the new life of marriage without any difficulties, knowing that the journey had just begun. We were in high spirits coming from our honeymoon in England, and the next day, we shared the great experience with loved ones who came to see us at home. With open arms, they welcomed us back to our native land. We felt the comforting presence of God in our home near the seacoast as folks from all over visited with us in the days that followed.

Elecia had two beautiful daughters, Nadine and Charmaine, prior to the union; and they immediately became my own daughters when we got married. They were angels of light sent from above to multiply our joy. From the day I met them, I knew that God had put them into my life from that moment onward. We tried our best to bring them up in the fear and admonition of the Lord Jesus Christ. The eldest one, Nadine, was nine years old; and Charmaine was only four years old when we began to live our lives together. They were beacons of light to us as we lived happily ever after near the skirt of the Blue Mountain in the seacoast town of Port Antonio.

Two years later, my wife was pregnant, and my joy was multiplied. I wanted a son, so I prayed earnestly toward that end. There was excitement

Our eldest daughter—Nadine, best-looking girl in town

Our younger daughter—Charmaine, wanted to be a movie star

in my bosom when I learned that we were going to have a baby. I waited patiently for the child to be born, not wanting to find out the sex of the baby before birth. In my heart, I knew that it would be a boy; and even though my wife challenged me about this daily, I stuck to my belief that she would have a son. I asked God for a son and believed that He was going to answer my prayer, so I kept hope in God that one day soon, my prayer will be answered on this matter. It was a time of great expectation as we waited for that day of revelation where our hearts will rejoice in the fullness of joy.

In August 1982, Elecia decided to visit New York in order to shop for the expected child who was about to come into our world very soon. I was convinced that it was a boy, so I was bent on buying clothes for a boy while she was concentrating on things pertaining to a girl baby. Unfortunately, she had to travel alone to New York because I was not yet granted a travel visa to the United States. This really broke my heart. I wanted to be close to her at all times, but circumstances beyond my control prevented me from traveling with her. I was a very much concerned about her leaving for New York without me. This was heartrending for me, but I took courage in the fact that she was going to stay with her sister Amoy, who was a nurse in New York. I watched from the waiting gallery with sadness as she departed on an Air Jamaica flight destined for the John F. Kennedy International Airport.

While she was abroad, my thoughts went out to her daily. There were times when I got worried, confused, and anxious about her and the unborn child. I began to pray and hope that everything was fine with my wife and baby. As the days and weeks passed by, I became more and more concerned for Elecia's welfare. We were thousands of miles apart, but our hearts and spirits were closer than ever. There were days when my aching heart burned with intense frustration as I pondered with great expectation, wanting her to return home sooner than she has planned. It was my worst nightmare, and being so far away from her for the first time since we got married brought much pain to me. However, I realized that I could not change the present situation despite of my frustrations.

The next four to six weeks were extremely difficult for me. Elecia got sick and could not return home as planned; she was admitted to the Elmhurst Hospital in Queens, New York. This caused a great amount of stress for me because now she had to be staying longer than anticipated. Each time she spoke to me on the telephone, I felt a little better, hearing her sweet voice from across the miles. Based upon the fact that she was hospitalized, she had to remain there under the doctor's observation; as a result of that, she was contemplating on having the baby in New York. I became more and more impatient as the days went by, especially when I heard that the baby was going to be born overseas. This, of course, was heartrending for me, not being able to be there in the labor room with my wife in that precious moment when my child comes into the world.

According to the doctors, the baby was due at the end of September or the beginning of October. It was now October 10, and my nerves were rocking with fear, knowing that anything was possible at this point. My sisters-in-law Dorrett and Janet were always there to encourage me in my moment of anxiety. They were towers of strength to me in those frightening hours of great expectation. My days began to get brighter with these two sisters encouraging me on in those days of doubts and fear, which gripped my life in that daunting autumn season. It was truly an experience for me, waiting for the news of the birth of my child.

On October 14, I came home from my job, at the Bonnie view Plantation Hotel took a short nap, and went to choir practice at church. At the end of the rehearsal, I requested prayer for my wife and unborn baby; the wonderful saints of God laid hands upon me as a point of contact and prayed for Elecia in New York. She was in the hospital, preparing for delivery. The folks at church encouraged me in the Lord, saying, "Do not worry, Brother Brown, God will take care of the situation." I left the church that night with great courage and a settled peace in my heart that everything was going to be all right. Those church folks lifted my spirit. I felt better than I was before the rehearsal. They had a warm, penetrating, and contagious love that allowed me to have courage in difficulties. So I went on my merry way, rejoicing, knowing that someone cared about my struggles.

As I journeyed home after choir practice, I started to feel some unusual pains all over my body. These pains came momentarily while I walked up the hill to King Street. Upon reaching home, I told Dorrett about the pains I was feeling; she remarked that I was helping my wife to bear the pains of childbirth. The pains intensified as the hours went by, and I knew that this was not normal, but I just couldn't explain how I felt. However, I tried to ignore the pains as much as possible, centering my thoughts overseas, pondering about my beloved wife and child. I spent most of the night thinking about them, before I eventually fell asleep.

The next day I took the day off from the job due to the increased pain all over my body. I waited anxiously to hear from Elecia that day, pacing the floor up and down for the most part. Suddenly, the telephone rang; it was three o'clock in the afternoon. Our eldest daughter, Nadine, answered the telephone; and she suddenly burst out with excitement, saying, "It's Mommy! She had a son!" Upon hearing this, I ran toward the telephone with frantic joy, anxiously awaiting my turn to speak.

Then Nadine quickly handed me the telephone. With stammering lips, I said "Hello, darling, are you ok?"

"Yes, honey," replied Elecia on the other end of the line. "God has answered your prayer, Aubrey. It's a boy," she added. I was jumping uncontrollably all over the room, praising God for answering my prayer for a son. My heart rejoiced after hearing the best news of the week and perhaps the best news ever.

A fresh breeze of jubilation began to blow in that house at 8 King Street that afternoon when my son was born. My heart was filled with gratitude and happiness. The entire family joined me in this great celebration of joy on that glorious day of gladness. My dream came true that afternoon when our son was born. I later learned that Elecia was in labor the same time I was feeling the pains all over my body. She named the baby Khavil. I wanted to name him Aubrey III, but Elecia insisted there were too many Aubrey in the family; so in the end, we both agreed to name him Khavil Aubrey Brown.

After getting the good news, I became more anxious to see them both. Elecia decided to return home within the next nine days after she gave birth to a bouncing baby boy. On October 24, they arrived at the Norman Manley International Airport in Kingston, Jamaica, West Indies, in fine style on an Air Jamaica flight—the most colorful airline in the world. My soul was soaring to new heights of uncontrollable ecstasy as I waited for that historic moment to come. When the aircraft landed, I was sitting at the waiting gallery with earnest expectation, waiting and looking for the first sight of my loved ones and to embrace my family in a glorious reunion. I looked with eager eyes, fixed on the entrance of the gangway of that Air Jamaica flight. It was a fairly good distance away, but I wanted to capture the first photograph of my son's appearing in the Land of Sunshine, Wood, and Water. Suddenly, I saw my wife and son coming down the staircase of the aircraft. It was raining heavily; one of the flight attendants assisted them with an umbrella and escorted them down the long and wet staircase. I literally counted every step she took to get to the bottom of the stairs and prayed that she would not slip and fall on the wet surface. I stood in the rain, looking on, refusing to move until Elecia took the final step and reached the bottom of the stairs safely.

After clearing Immigration and Customs, they came outside the terminal building where I was waiting. Excitement permeated the atmosphere as we hugged and kissed like we were losing our minds. It was a glorious reunion for all of us on that day of arrival. Some folks steared at us; others smiled. It seemed as if we have transformed the airport terminal into a citadel of praise to the highest God. We began to worship Jehovah, thanking Him for having brought my family home safely. After this, we drove away, leaving some onlookers standing in awe as we departed the scene for home. It was a joy to be together again to share and express our feelings for each other and to celebrate the birth of a newborn baby boy, whom I called the Son of my Vision.

When we reached home at 8 King Street, the celebration began as family and friends gathered to rejoice with us for the gift of our newborn son, Khavil Aubrey. His sisters, Nadine and Charmaine, were filled with excitement; and each took turns holding him. Our joy was multiplied, and our hearts rejoiced in the god of grace on that evening of October when God looked down from heaven and smiled on our family. From there on, we spent our lives as a tale that is told that generation to come might venture upon its plot and be encouraged by the thoughts that they too can overcome all obstacles that may present themselves in the onward march of life. Therefore, it was incumbent upon us to give thanks to the great and mighty God for the unmerited blessings bestowed upon us.

The struggles had affected my life—emotionally, mentally, and spiritually. There are negative and positive results that linger with me for the most part of my journey to the brighter side of life. I have crossed many oceans of turmoil, tunneled mountains, and walked through the valley of the shadow of death in my quest for a brighter tomorrow. After the storms of life devastated the various areas of my life, I sought refuge in the god of my deliverance, who rescued my soul from hell and planted my feet on higher ground. The fullness of time came when God delivered me from my heavy burdens and set me on my way rejoicing. My journey of agony ended, and the bells of joy rang once again within my sacred bosom. And

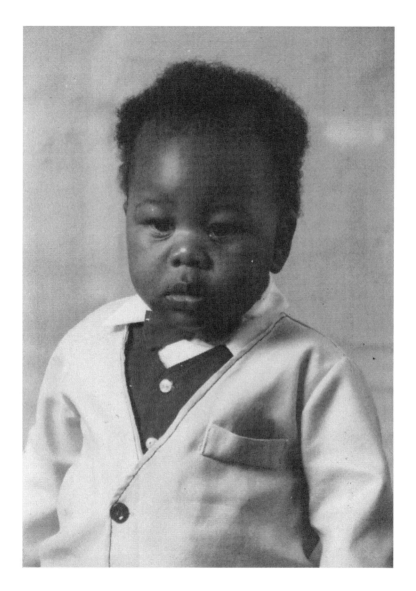

Khavil Aubrey—the son of my vision

from there on, my family and I lived happily ever after, contending for the faith of Jesus Christ as we continue to proclaim the good news of salvation as the only hope for a dying world.

Now our minds are made up, our visions are clear, and we are cognizant of the fact that it was the good Lord up above that has taken us to this point of our lives. Therefore, we will rejoice in Him and be glad for "hitherto has the Lord helped us," and we are eternally grateful to God and all others who have touched our lives one way or the other. The journey I took was a long and troublesome one, filled with persecution, trials, and crosses. But each step of the way was guided by the Holy Spirit. We have overcome the onslaughts of the enemy, climbed the mountains of victories, and now are pressing our way toward the portals of the heavenly city—the New Jerusalem, where we shall spend our long eternity.

Now that the great conflict is over, the struggle is erased from the contents of my journey. The god of all grace has lavished me with unquenched love that is undeserving. The unmerited favor of Jehovah has been with me on my journey to the onward march of life. Therefore, it is imperative that I pause long enough to extol the Master of the universe for His extraordinary design in the development and advancement of my life over these many years of Christian warfare. The struggles were sometimes seemingly unbearable as the quest to discover more of God became the central truth of my ecclesiastical and theological investigation. The more I inquired from the scriptures, the more I found out that my finite intellect could not withstand the magnitude of such vast, magnificent, and captivating data of the infinite God. Therefore, I am left to think that I am but a simple creature and nothing but folly without God.

There are other struggles that I must face and more burdens to bear on my journey to the other side of life, but I will be content in whatsoever state. I know that the journey I take will soon end. There is a river of clear water over the horizon that beckons me to drink until my thirst is quenched. With this in mind, I will press toward the coveted prize ahead with vigor and with virtue. Then my heart will go on singing, with joy I will carry on the Master's work from the dawn to the evening's twilight when day is done and night is past. Now I must labor on with sweet assurance of entering the celestial city at the end of my Christian journey when the day dawns upon my smiling brow and the shadows of this unkind world shall flee away.

The effects of the struggles

All my children—Nadine, Charmaine, & K-Aubrey

Elecia and I—living happily ever after

ABOUT THE AUTHOR

Dr. Aubrey C. H. Brown Jr. is a son of the beautiful country of Jamaica, West Indies. He was born in Portland, the most salubrious part of the country. In his formative years, he attended the Bound Brook Infant School and the Port Antonio Primary School. Dr. Brown later attended the Port Antonio Senior School and the Aboukir Educational and Industrial Institute in St. Ann, Jamaica; he is a graduate of Bethel Bible College, Mandeville, Jamaica, with a diploma in theology and a bachelor degree in theology.

He continued his quest for knowledge and enrolled at Stratford Career Institute, Washington DC, where he graduated with a diploma in hotel management with the highest honors. Dr. Brown is a graduate of Church of God School of Evangelism, Cleveland, Tennessee, and Billy Graham International School of Evangelism, Minneapolis, Minnesota, with certificates in evangelism. He is also a graduate of Anchor Theological Seminary, with a master of theology and a doctorate degree in theology with the highest honors as the Most Outstanding Student of the Year and the valedictorian of his class.

Dr. Brown has served as chairman and board member of various religious and civic organizations, including school boards, HIV committees, sports committees, and cultural and community organizations. He also served as dean and lecturer at Bethel Bible College-Port Antonio campus for over three years, chaplain of the Castle police station, marriage officer, secretary of the Governor-General Prayer Vigil Committee, secretary for the Billy Graham International Crusade, chairman of the Portland Expo religious affairs committee, secretary for the "Bible and the Ball" committee, production assistant for the movie, "the mighty Quinn" chairman and secretary of the Portland Ministers Fraternal, a member the New York State Church of God Youth Board, and an ordained bishop of the Church of God, Cleveland, Tennessee. He is the recipient of numerous awards and commendations.

Dr. Brown is a pastor, poet, and songwriter, play-write, scout, and is currently working on twelve books; he is presently the pastor of the Showers of Blessing Church of God in Uniondale, New York.

He is married to the *girl of his dreams*, Elecia, with whom he has three wonderful children, who later gave them six brilliant, lovely, and energetic grandchildren. Dr. Brown enjoys country music, sports, cooking, travelling, and writing.